The Tompo of the Ringing

The Tompo of the Ringing

Tracy Santa

East of the Mountains and West of the Sun

RHYOLITE PRESS LLC
Colorado Springs, Colorado

Santa, Tracy
The Tompo of the Ringing
1st edition April 1, 2022

Foreword: Copyright © 2021 Warren Zanes

ISBN 978-1-943829-41-5
Library of Congress Control Number: 2022933728

Publisher's Cataloging-in-Publication data

Names: Santa, S. Tracy, 1954-, author. | Zanes, Warren, foreword author.
Title: The tompo of the ringing : a rock and roll memoir / by Tracy Santa; foreword by Warren Zanes.
Description: Colorado Springs, CO: Rhyolite Press, 2022.
Identifiers: LCCN: 2022933728 | ISBN: 9781943829415
Subjects: LCSH Santa, S. Tracy, 1954-. | Musicians--Biography. | Rock musicians--United States--Biography. | BISAC BIOGRAPHY & AUTOBIOGRAPHY / Music | BIOGRAPHY & AUTOBIOGRAPHY / Personal Memoirs
Classification: LCC ML420 .S26 S26 2022 | DDC 784/.092--dc23

Cover design, book design/layout by Donald R. Kallaus

Published in the United States of America by Rhyolite Press, LLC
P.O. Box 60144
Colorado Springs, Colorado 80960
www.rhyolitepress.com

To Bebe and Maggie,
music lovers.

CONTENTS

ACT III

I don't know what it is
Or what it can do
But I've got to find me
A ring dang doo

—Sam "the Sham" Samudio
& the Pharaohs

I can't quite remember
what it was that I knew

—Neil Young "They Might Be Lost"

FOREWORD

I've noticed that many of those who gave themselves to rock and roll didn't get a lot in return. The rock and roll lifestyle could be unforgiving, promising nothing . . . and often making good on that promise. What rock and roll did offer, whether you played clubs, stadiums, or backyards, was stories. And every band generally had one or two members ready and able to tell them. Maybe it was the result of long drives between gigs, long silences between songs, or just the age-old thing of wanting to leave a painting on the cave wall after the kill.

What I've also witnessed over the years is that rock and roll stories tend to hinge on the detail. Some arguably insignificant element in the narrative becomes the center, the fulcrum. The detail could be that the drummer wore three pairs of underwear at gigs because his ass would sweat so much when his group played their extended version of "Hang on Sloopy." *Tell Sloopy Three Pair*. Or, it could be, the guitar player's nose, which needed blowing, on the night in Worcester when he attempted to negotiate payment with a drunken club owner known for underworld ties. *Tell Worcester Nose blow*. In the process through which rock and roll memories become rock and roll stories, the detail becomes the key. I have no theory as to why this is the case, I only know that I want more of these things. All I can get, really.

Tracy Santa's, *The Tompo of the Ringing* is a book of details. The band members come and go. The band names change. The cities and towns blur one into the next. It's a series of disappearances, whether we're talking drummers and girlfriends, good ideas, or moments of artistic transcendence. It all comes and goes. But in the wake of those disappearances, details remain and from them stories have been constructed. I feel sure the ones here have been told many times among a small group of people. But it's those fragments in them, so abundant, that lend this volume what is in my mind its almost Homeric quality. Read this book and know the man's journey . . . *because* of the details. I think of the scar on Odysseus's thigh, seen by the nursemaid washing his leg, the woman who knew him as a boy. That scar becomes a story within a story, another tale to be told, built on the strength of a single detail.

That said, I'm not sure if the hero in these pages ever finds his home or his family, as Odysseus did. The man here certainly keeps looking for both, repeatedly playing "Wooly Bully" with the next set of clowns he'll call "my band." But let's hope it's about the journey and not the destination, because this hero is not likely to arrive anywhere finally and forever. But some part of me, surely the rock and roll part, loves this man's capacity to keep searching, to try again, to form that next group. I'm sure he's lost count of the bands he's been in. But on he goes, lowering his expectations as he makes his way. The electrician who stops by to handle some wiring issue: if he can form an E chord, he might just find himself in a group before getting back in his truck. Tracy Santa never needed the members of Toto to back him—expertise was not the thing he was after. All he wanted was for you to stay in the room with him for a few hours, weeks, months, and try, just try. Don't leave him alone there.

* * *

I met Tracy Santa in a place of darkness, New Orleans, LA. I was there to hit some kind of bottom, not knowing that this was the reason most people were there. I hadn't planned it that way, of course. Neither had they. But if truth-in-advertising was the priority, the logo for New Orleans would be the downward spiral. A city of heavy breathing and excuses for being late, its bars were very busy. If I didn't meet Tracy in one of them, we made our way there minutes later. Miss Mae's. The Brothers Three (which we cleverly called Tres Hermanos). The town was decorated in cheap drinks. But when it came to having stories to tell, New Orleans was and is the envy of all America.

Tracy was a buoyant figure on the scene, a laughing man. But his disguise was one of the city's best. Though grinning his way past shotgun shacks, he wasn't actually buoyant a few layers in. He was kind, energetic, capable of great and well-crafted mischief, encouraging, creative, empathetic, boisterous, loud. He was also wrestling with some force down inside. Fortunately for us, he preferred that it come out in song. He was, I would come to realize, a man who needed his music. We shared that. And it became a bond for life. That's how I got the job writing this foreword.

Have I been speaking of Tracy in the past tense? Apologies. I think literary convention took me there. Or perhaps I like a pulpit and the opportunity to memorialize a friend. But he's alive. And he wants you in his next band.

* * *

One time Tracy came to my Magazine St. apartment with Alex Chilton, a German fellow named Wolfgang, and a beautiful young woman, Kathleen. It was the afternoon, and I had been sleeping. They knocked on my door, suspecting that I had some pot. I did. But I was out of rolling papers. Somehow they all knew that Kathleen had "feminine napkins," so papers were fashioned from the outer packaging. Little thought was given to Kathleen's comfort through all this. I think she was wondering how she ended up in this position. I also think I saw her eyeing the door. But she was there because she'd attended Alex's show at Tipitina's the night before and the night wasn't over. It was just another day in New Orleans. I lived with Kathleen for a few years after that. That's how I remember the city in that period in my life. I was involved in an experiment: I wanted to see if I could stretch my teenage years out so far that they'd cover all of my twenties.

I had one fight with Tracy during that period, an argument about music and how it should be recorded. I was being fastidious in a studio, slow and deliberate, wanting to make a recording like Jeff Lynne made recordings, without knowing how to do it. Tracy was from the think-too-long-kill-the-song school. The Beatles made a record in a day, he'd say, and I hadn't even gotten a guitar sound. I heard shit along those lines, and I believe it was appropriate. In that moment, however, we could barely see one another from the opposite ends of the spectrum. Tracy got a little fed up and let some feelings loose in the room. I did the same. The next morning there was an apology note and a box outside my door. The front of the note was a photograph of a soul food restaurant, with a sign in the restaurant's window saying, "Brains 15 cents." On the back it said, "Sorry." The box was a case of wine, MD 20/20, Wild Irish Rose, all the worst stuff. That was the last of it, never discussed again. And we drank it all.

Meaning, we didn't spend our time together talking about feelings. Neither did we drift toward the bookstore's self-help section. We were after something along the lines of Bukowski, which, when we got our hands on it, we'd read as a how-to manual. Our time was given to more pressing questions, such as, "Would it be possible to record a whole album in the women's room at Berry Park?" Or "The Kinks?" Or, at still greater philosophical heights, "Do you know what time this place closes?" But we did have feelings, and I'd say we were tangled in them as we went looking for a guitar cord that worked.

* * *

One odd thing about Tracy in that New Orleans period was that he was a professor. In fact, he was a professor at the university I was attending. It felt strange passing him in the hallways in and around the Loyola University English Dept. What species was he? Faculty? Student? We'd been drinking Early Times bourbon just four hours prior, and he was wearing the same clothes. Was "Hello, Professor Santa" the right thing to say? When he approached me for Advil, should I respond or just keep walking?

I imagined it was a curious predicament for him, to be a faculty member but hanging around with students. Even if I was an "older student" and pretty fresh off five years of road work with The Del Fuegos. I didn't let on to other faculty members that Tracy led a double life. My ignorance kept me from seeing the truth right in front of me, though: he wasn't leading a double life. He thought little of it, had nothing to hide. He just wanted to have a rock and roll band, and university campuses were littered with kids who could almost form barre chords. He drove a tiny car, was often sweating a lot, and never once said no to playing a little music. Professor Santa wasn't actually looking to conceal anything *or* change anything.

This book could have a Part II. I hope it does. None of the stuff we did is in here. Come to think of it, maybe there shouldn't be a Part II. But I celebrate Part I. And I'll say this: in reading it I learned more than I was prepared for about a friend I *thought* I knew. I recognized some of the details, here and there, but the shock came in just how many of these stories I hadn't heard. A number of them involve cold automobiles in bad weather, small apartments with several males and one bed, unfortunate smells, instruments being sold at pawn shops—things I know I would have complained about in my own life both when they were happening and after. But Tracy relished it all, then and now.

He's always treated each rock and roll moment like a precious thing. He's the guy smiling when someone throws a drink on the band and tells them to go home, forever. "We're really doing it!" The details, the beautiful specifics and the madness involved, these are the collectibles he's been moving with him from town to town, in boxes that have filled shitty cars, no way to see out the rearview mirror. I'm glad he's finally taken it all down off his shelves, pulled it all out from those boxes, spread it across his living room floor, his kitchen and the hallway, out the front door, into the street, laying it down so he can see it all, show it to us, spreading it across towns and cities, every place he's ever been, over mountains and oceans, letting it all go where good stories go and keep going.

—Warren Zanes,
  November, 2021

ACT I

POINT OF INFORMATION

My home town was founded in 1650 at the confluence of the Housa-tonic and Naugatuck Rivers as a trading post trafficking in wolf hides. The land was purchased from the Paugussett Indian Nation in 1662. Who knows how much the English colonists paid, but the Paugussett and Potatucks moved north. In my youth, we played Little League baseball on top of a Potatuck graveyard in Riverside Park. The town, founded as Ripton parish of Stratford then established as Hunting-ton in 1789—after Samuel Huntington, appointed to the Connecti-cut Supreme Court of Errors in 1773—recorded 2040 adults and 120 slaves in the 1790 U.S. census. Huntington's upcountry Yankee hard rock farmers and downtown river-hugging factory workers re-incor-porated as Shelton in 1919, branding the town in honor of Edward Shelton, canal builder and local grandee of industry. My stock was of the factory folk. In 1975 Shelton was the site of the largest arson fire in U.S. history. The old B.F. Goodrich tire plant, a quarter-mile long, three-story, Dickensian brick sweathouse, was lit up under the spon-sorship of its absentee owner, Charles Moeller, president of Ohio's Grant Sheet Metal Products. Moeller escaped criminal prosecution but was later convicted by jury in civil court and held libel in 1988.

The Boys' Club Bus

Repeat after me, to the tune of Chris Montez's "Let's Dance"

> *Come on baby/Let's take a chance*
> *Left my rubbers/In my other pants*

Or to the tune of Sam the Sham and the Pharoahs' "Ring Dang Do"

> *You can have your jizz/And your rubbers, too*
> *All I want/Is a lay from you*

Not your style? Then comp to this ditty, following the lead of the Beatles' "All My Loving."

> *Close your eyes/Spread your legs*
> *And I'll fertilize/Your eggs*

Enough choral singing for now—we've just finished sixth grade, and our bus is pulling up in front of the Shelton Boys' Club.

Wild in the Streets

I was not a wild child. I went to church every Sunday and to cate-chism class after school on Tuesdays. I got good grades, went to con-fession, was absolved of my venial sins, and obeyed my parents and teachers, mostly. But when we camped out in the backyard, we would strip buck naked and roam for miles around town in the middle of the night.

Why, you ask? We weren't naturists. We didn't under normal conditions in the light of day find clothes a burden. We were as accustomed as the next set of citizens to putting on our uniforms each morning. It's just that—unsupervised and on our own, like rolling stones—we elected to get out on the town in the altogether.

We had our reasons, I guess. One challenge was to skinny dip in the backyard pool of a certain female classmate. It was a pre-adoles-cent form of counting coup. We would stealthily approach our objec-tive, crawling on our bellies, then boost ourselves over the side of a low chain link fence, slip into the water, and perform a few gentle breast strokes, quickly slipping out, greased seals, running off down the road, shriveled doodles airing in the night air.

Running down the middle of the road bare-ass was electric, the pavement still warm on our feet from the summer sun. When the moon was out, the world was bright, sharply outlined. We could see everything, and no one saw us. Houses were completely dark, seemingly uninhabited. Dogs slept, Kellman's barn leaned into the night humidity, full to the rafters with early summer hay. Out in the country you could hear a car half a mile away, its lights slowly coming into focus. We'd sprint off the road and tumble into the weeds, the car louder and brighter, then passing and fading into the night. One night after a midnight dip we lifted a street sign with its heavy metal pole and trotted with it half a mile down the road. We pulled a second street sign from its lodging, implanted the sign and pole we'd lugged down the road, retraced our steps carrying the newly purloined sign back to the original site of larceny, and planted it. We were out to sow confusion, no?

Baby dada steps. No harm, no foul, no clothes. No clue.

Every Night at Ten

My first guitar was a plastic guitar, Xmas 1965. A prototype plastic guitar was designed in the 1930s by Mario Maccaferri, an Italian guitar instructor and luthier living in London. Maccaferri aspired to manufacture serious plastic instruments—he later designed plastic clarinet reeds used by Benny Goodman—but the world toyed with Maccaferri's dream.

Consequently, my Tiger guitar was manufactured by Emenee, toy makers. The Tiger was cherry caramel colored and came in a tiger-striped cardboard carrying case. The package included a small, battery powered amp. I sat on the back porch that summer, playing one string accompaniment to the Animals' "It's My Life," singing along with Eric Burden

Girl there are ways/To make certain things pay.

One string guitar wasn't going to cut the limelight, so I first attempted to make my mark playing a silver tambourine, singing falsetto vocals in our neighborhood's first iteration of a garage band. I'd talk my way into practices in Greg White's basement, but once it was clear that background vocals on the Small Faces' "Little Tin Soldier" were the pinnacle of my contribution, I became expendable. It wouldn't have crossed my mind to take a lead vocal, nor was anyone asking. I was like someone trying to earn a varsity letter as the back-up holder for the second string placekicker.

I saved $20 from a month of picking strawberries and at the end of the summer bought a guitar of Japanese origin and no discernible brand. The blue guitar seemed made of ironwood. It was ill-used and literally the cheapest guitar hanging among the hundreds of guitars dangling from the ceiling of Banko's House of Music. I could slide my hand between the strings and neck without much effort, a feature which worked against actually fretting the guitar and producing a distinct note. It was a difficult guitar to play and sounded it, in my hands. I used the guitar to play bass, one painful note at a time. Chords were beyond my technical or theoretical capacity.

My first band consisted of other Rookie League types. We were all in seventh-grade at Elizabeth Shelton Middle School. Our lead guitarist was an unassuming classmate I'd known since first grade who had just come out the closet as a guitarist. Janet sat down while she played a big, hollow-bodied electric, something you'd expect Wes Montgomery to pull out of his gig bag. Bobbie B. played an early 60's off-brand surf guitar with four pick-ups, three of which seemed merely decorative. Ricky Ziegler, with perfect Ricky Nelson hair, also played guitar, and we all shared Janet and Bobbie's small Kent amps. Mark Kiley posed as our singer. Mark departed from our life after seventh-grade, and aside from his bowl-cut hair and Crazy Guggenheim smile, what I recall of Mark is that his parents bought his brother a urinal for his college dorm, for Christmas. We rehearsed in Ricky's parents' living room, which had a piano. Mark once tried to play "House of the Rising Sun" on it, unsuccessfully. That a group of white seventh-graders might not be positioned to play a song about the bonds and wages of prostitution in turn-of-the-century New Orleans never crossed our minds. Everyone played "House of the Rising Sun," so we tried too.

Janet could in fact play guitar quite well, but she could not rock. It had not been part of the lesson plan in her guitar school. She just could not get her mojo working, nor even identify where it was located. Not that the rest of us were in touch with our mojo, nor any notion of how we might operate our mojo should we stumble on it by accident. Nor could we competently keep a 4/4 beat or tune our guitars in unison. That aside, we were short but a drummer of getting a cherished gig at a St. Paul's Church dance.

By the time our seventh-grade band regrouped at the beginning of eighth-grade for a run at the big time, we had downsized. Janet was gone, Mark had migrated, Bobbie and Ricky remained on guitar. Given that I was still only capable of playing one note at a time, I traded my ironwood six-string and $35 at Banko's House of Music for a Zim-Gar bass. The Zim-Gar's chief selling point was that it had not been pre-ruined by another acolyte of the one-string bass run. And it was an actual bass, with four fat strings—much easier to play than a six string guitar passing as a bass.

The origins of the Zim-Gar brand are obscure. What was Zim-Gar short for? A piscine bottom-feeder? It was neither sold out of a Sears' catalogue nor available at Woolworth's. While this was a dubious distinction, it was a distinction nonetheless. The Zim-Gar featured a racy sunburst finish, a stylish brown pickguard, and a half scale neck designed for a dwarf. Its Japanese origin, in 1968, was not a mark of distinct craftsmanship.

But it was new. And with it I gained a little stage experience, playing the Zim-Gar behind friend Jaime at his cousin's birthday party cousin at the Beacon Falls VFW Hall. The bass line to "In the Midnight Hour" was still beyond me, over the horizon in an indeterminate future of dreamed competency. I faked Duck Dunn's funky line by playing half the notes in all the time. We practiced for the gig in the kitchen of Jaime's house, as the kitchen was the only room with two electrical outlets. The smell of tomato sauce was affixed to the wallpaper. Drummer Bobby slicked his blonde hair back. It was 1968, but the Sixties were still a rumor in our moribund factory town.

With our primary band, we now enlisted our buddy Freddie Kekacs on drums. Freddie was a dead ringer for Ringo in 1962, when Ringo still sported a ducktail. Our plan for success was calculating and sure-fire. We would become the band who would find a singer who would enunciate the *actual* lyrics to "Louie, Louie."

No junior high band of substance played a set in 1967 without including "Louie, Louie." But who dared sing the actual lyrics?

Every night at ten/I lay her again

At least these were purported to be the actual lyrics. The Kingsmen had mumbled through their hypnotic, atrociously recorded version of Richard Berry's song, purposefully obscuring these and other, even *more* salacious lyrics. That the song was a huge AM radio hit proved that you could fool at least some of the FCC censors some of the time. Taking a cue from Kingsman Jack Ely's marble-mouthed delivery, every garage band in our neck of the woods slurred their way through "Louie, Louie's" litany of teenage kicks.

The real lyrics of the Kingmen's "Louie Louie" were tough to pin down. It was a guild thing, in a way—you needed to apprentice to a mentor skilled in the art of dowsing for unlawful carnal lyrics. It would have been tough for any one of us in the band to convincingly offer up the lyric, even if we had been privy to its code. Maybe Freddie, but he wouldn't sing. The notion of laying her again was a bit beyond our experiential grasp. Laying her once would have been nice, though we would have needed an operator's manual to get started. And in any case, and as to every night at ten, most of us were not permitted out of the house after ten. Courting a singer who would actually articulate the precise nuances of "Louie, Louie" was an act of conscious transgression on our part, but we desperately needed something to give us an edge in the violent competition for a slot at a St. Paul's hop.

I knew a man up to the task. Ronnie Lynseed was blessed with not one but two older brothers who were card-carrying juvenile delinquents. Ronnie's idea of spectator sport was to peek through the knot in his bedroom floor, directly over the downstairs toilet, watching his younger sister pee. I'd first met Ronnie when I was in kindergarten. He lived across the street from my buddy Paul Marshalka, and would stand on the side of the road imploring us to cross the thoroughfare to come and play with him. Is that a boy or a girl, I asked Paul. Boy, I think, Paul said. At the age of four, Ronnie had a full-on Little Lord Fauntleroy do, a pre-incarnation of Brian Jones, five years ahead of his time.

By eighth grade, Ronnie had become our one-man *Joy of Sex*. He could go on for hours about what good fortune had befallen him at the campground in Rhode Island his family had staked out for three weeks as his brothers were cut loose to wreak havoc in an adjoining state's legal jurisdiction.

Ronnie's most illuminating lesson, for our money, was his chronicle of double-decker fucking. Ronnie's neighbor Hugh and I were all ears. Single-decker fucking, after all, seemed sufficient to our needs.

Ronnie set the table for us. "I was fucking this girl in our tent and there was this other guy I met. His girlfriend and him were fucking right next to us," Ronnie casually confided.

Right, we nodded. This was the most regular occurrence we could imagine.

"So we were rolling around. And you're not going to believe this— his chick ended up under my chick. I was on top of them *both*."

Of course, we concurred. What else could be more likely? Happens all the time when you're camping out with your family in Rhode Island.

"All of a sudden—I was fucking this chick, and *my prick came right out of her ass.*

Big prick that Ronnie has we silently surmised.

"*I came right out the other side of her.* Can you guys believe that? And my dick—this is unbelievable, but *my dick* slipped into—*her friend's cunt*! I swear to God—I was fucking *both of them* at the same time."

"You're shitting me!"

"I shit you not."

Hugh and I chewed on this image for a moment. The shish-kabob theory of sexual intercourse strongly intrigued us. We were laughing ourselves silly about it, for sure, but not so much in incredulity as in envy. What a wonderful world this would be, if we could all just relax with a little more double-decker fucking.

Ronnie was clearly the guy to deliver "Louie Louie's" goods. If this seventh-grade cocksman—a year younger than us, on top of everything and everyone—couldn't deliver truth to the powers of St. Paul, who could? We scheduled a couple of rehearsals with Ronnie. He was happy to be singing with us, though we were a bit surprised to find he couldn't carry a tune to save the rainforest, and he wasn't much good at remembering song lyrics either. That was fine. We shifted to Plan B, where Ronnie mostly banged the tambourine before his feature presentation.

We also found he was not very good at remembering the lyrics to "Louie Louie," but we encouraged him to simply repeat the good parts, very clearly.

"Remember, Ronnie: '*Every night at ten/I lay her again*'." Ronnie smiled, nodding sagely. This was a concept Ronnie could get his arms around.

We secured the St. Paul's gig on our clean looks and relentless whining, strategically failing to mention our new lead singer, who was considerably more hirsute and disheveled than the rest of us. We must have been opening for a more competent and heralded group of teenage musicians, e.g. The Myddle Class, where friend Chuck held forth on accomplished lead guitar.

The St. Paul's rec hall was dimly lit, the wooden stage low. The refreshment table to the rear of the small hall held glass bottles of Cott soda and Dixie cups. Chaperones patrolled discreetly in the shadows. We ran our short set—the Monkees' "Last Train to Clarksville," the

Larry Williams-by-Beatles-by-Young Rascals hit "Slow Down," Wilson Pickett's "Midnight Hour," an hour of the day few of us had ever seen. Then it was time for Ronnie to testify through the Kustom PA system to what happened every night at ten.

We were tingling with the danger of it all. What would happen? Would the chaperones turn on the overhead lights mid-song, revealing junior high couples frantically fondling on fold-out metal chairs in every corner of the room? Would our restrained, proper, church-going female classmates be driven to a lather, unhinged by Ronnie's audacity, hip-thrusting in a mini-skirt mating frenzy? Would my girlfriend Belinda, so amply endowed for a woman of her tender age, stare at me—her one and only—in new and knowing ways, imagining the fresh discoveries we would now make the next time we embraced in the weeds down by the abandoned gravel pit?

Yes—we offered up "Louie Louie." But the sky did not fall, nor did the walls of the temple crumble, nor were members of the audience turned to pillars of salt in their tracks, nor was there evidence of spontaneous erotic combustion. Who knows what sensations "Louie Louie" stirred in the hearts and loins of young men and women that evening? The air documented our moment and it drifted out of the room. The facts? Ronnie sang "Louie Louie," no more clearly than it had been sung a dozen times previously in the Youth Hall Center, second floor, St. Paul's Church Annex. Perhaps our version might have been less fully realized than some. We were all learning on the job, and when Ronnie strayed beyond personal narrative, he kind of lost focus.

I don't think we played again with Ronnie. Not that we were

disappointed with his performance, or with each other, nor were we suffering artistic differences, nor were any of us entering rehab, nor running off with the Children of God, nor suffering other maladies smiting rock bands of our era. I guess we just peaked. Where do you go after you've played St. Paul's? None of us had an answer to that question. We tacitly agreed to separately pursue our eighth grade lives of quiet desperation, hiding our erections in our pockets after slow dances and setting off the occasional stink bomb on "A" floor of Fowler School.

The last time I saw Ronnie I had picked him up hitchhiking on a midwinter's day near the center of our town. I hadn't seen him in five years. I'd been away at college. Now I was a college dropout with a dead-end job and a $200 car. This put me about $200 ahead of Ronnie.

"Ronnie! My man. How's it hanging?"

Ronnie, with a full, late Jim Morrison beard, had put on a little weight.

"*Every night at ten, I lay her again,*" Ronnie quipped, swinging himself into the passenger seat.

"Enough about your sister. What you been up to?"

He said he'd worked for Beard Construction a while, pushing cement, but now he was retired. That's a plan, we agreed. I asked Ronnie to lock his door—he'd fallen out of his father's moving car once as a kid, and there was nothing secure about the passenger side door on my vehicle.

Ronnie had made 20. To the best of my knowledge, he remains happily retired.

People Can You Feel It?

The summer before high school, I took my June profits from truck farm labor and bought a used Hagstrom bass for $30. Hagstroms were Swedish guitars with soft, facile action. The bass was well-traveled when I acquired it. Its original red Corvette finish had acquired two different varieties of paisley wallpaper, in either an attempted upgrade or a willful act of vandalism. A peace symbol was deeply etched into its pickguard. With no amplifier but my battery-operated Tiger model, I was compelled to strip the Tiger guitar cord of its RCA jack, exposing the wires, and wrapped those exposed wires around the guitar cord jack plugged into the Hagstrom bass. A glorious fuzz tone resulted for the next forty seconds, at which point the Tiger speaker blew in a flap of smoking dissonance.

My father had received a Greco acoustic guitar for Christmas. There really is a Santa Claus, as I have no idea who else would have delivered this particular gift to this particular man. It wasn't as if my father was disinterested in music-making. He sometimes picked at my grandmother's piano late in the day at holiday gatherings. And I'd found an iron fife in the toy box in the basement a few years before. My father had apparently donned a tricorn hat and marched in a fife and drum corps in his teenage years. But my father—unlike his own

Hungarian-born tenor banjo strumming father—had never shown an inclination toward stringed instruments, nor did he much acquire an inclination after this gift. He was quite content to bang out standards on my sister's toy piano in the basement, always in the middle of the night, alone.

The Greco, while posing as a Spanish guitar, was like the Zim-Gar a product of Japanese craftsmanship. I bought a Mel Bay guitar instruction book and began the painful process of learning chords in my spare time, which was copious. Chords as diagrammed in Mel Bay were referred to by my fellow rock and roll apprentices as "the baby chords." Barre chords—in which you ran the basic E-chord claw up and down a guitar's neck to cover the scale—were clearly a more virile and manly method of producing a major chord. Barre chords were the very stuff of rock. All the strings, all the time, full-on loud.

I was far from ready for prime time as a guitarist, but as high school began my more musically accomplished buddies took a flying leap and invited me and Jim Stellar into their new aggregation as the rhythm section, drums and bass. I'd met Jim in an eighth grade gym class, which pitted the four-eyed eggheads (e.g. me) against the town's more hardened cases in sports of all varieties.

Stellar's story was that he was standing out in front of his house one day as a young boy. A motorcyclist comes ripping up Long Hill Avenue. With a baby on his bike. Was the baby simply lodged between his dad, the cyclist, and the sissy bar? Was he precariously balanced on the gas tank, like a little stunt devil? Just as this cyclist and tot rider approach Stellar, a car pulls out of the country lane feeding into Long Hill Avenue. The cyclist swerves, but too late. The car T-bones the cycle and cyclists, sending the leather-clad dad skidding across the pavement and launching his tiny passenger high in the air. The baby is in fact launched so high by the impact that it clears the telephone wires running alongside the road, a horrific, stupendous midget toss. Gravity intercedes and the bundle falls to the ground at Stellar's feet. The baby is dead. Stellar spends the next two years being home-schooled by his mom.

This tale was recounted on occasion to serve as an indirect and unembellished explanation of how Stellar became Stellar.

Stellar was not a good drummer, but he was a powerful drummer. His primitive wallop lacked technique, finesse, and steady time, thus mirroring my own skill set on bass. We rehearsed in Hugh's basement, down among his father's collection of handwritten pornography. None of us imagined this was the product of the mind or experience of Hugh's dad, a mild guy with a short gray flattop. We did think he might have been the copyist, but the handwriting looked too neat. We discovered no cursive manuscripts of *Lady Chatterley's Lover* or *The Story of O*, despite dogged digging in the stacks. The stories were direct and basic, the equivalent of 8mm stag films. Sort of like Stellar's drumming.

Among the five of us in the band, there were three real musicians, then Stellar and I. Hugh was serious. He could stand on one leg and play flute like Ian Anderson. We did several Tull songs (first album, pre-*Fatty* Martin Barre, pre-*Aqualung*) to capitalize on this talent. Robbie, who was once the best drummer we knew, was now the best guitarist we knew. He'd committed the Who's *Tommy* in its entirety to memory and figured out both guitar parts of the Allman Brothers'

"Revival," teaching the second part to George, who took this instruction grudgingly. George was a quick study and was in truth as good a guitarist as Robbie, but he lacked the high seriousness necessary to committing albums to memory and figuring out intricate arpeggios. George's idea of a good time was to break into Jimmy Page's manic solo on "Communication Breakdown" whenever a moment of relative silence presented itself during rehearsals. Stellar and I would join in, a half second, half beat, and half note off, trotting behind like troglodytes following our clan leader. Our idiot glee in performing a shard of a Led Zeppelin riff in a manner which almost rendered the song identifiable was unsurpassed, though not shared by our more task-driven band mates. When George broke into the riff for the fifth time in two hours, Robbie just rolled his eyes, and Hugh stared George down in his best Daltrey-attempting-to-discipline Townsend style.

What flipped Hugh's switch, however, was "Ramblin' Rose." I'd harangued Hugh into buying the first MC5 album at Bradlee's, and he was soon to regret the $3.98 he'd dropped on the Motor City 5. It ended up in my hands within days as work of insufficient merit, and consequently, a perfect match for my sensibilities and talent. But with clandestine exposure, I had infected certain members of our fraternity with a degraded immunity to trash. If George was willing to whip out an MC5 riff, we were on a slippery slope. I secretly hoped for a conversion experience, that Hugh might drop his guard, lower his standards, and jump in with a facsimile of Rob Tyner's Drano-gargling falsetto. When George finally thrashed out the opening power chords to MC5's anthem late one afternoon, we'd crossed the Rubicon of good taste. Too much monkey business for Hugh to be involved in. He stomped upstairs, leaving us chastened in the basement with buzzing Silvertone amps and a vast cache of handwritten pornography.

We hastily composed our 14 year-old selves and played a version of Cat Mother and the All-Night Newsboys' "Can You Dance to It?" This was a slab of sloppy whiteboy funk that even Stellar and I could get behind and push. We had to show Hugh that we were not pathetically dependent on his talents as vocalist and one-legged flautist. One song was enough to accomplish this, in our minds.

We were kind of embarrassed to be down in Hugh's basement without him. If we were playing, at least he knew we weren't tearing through boxes and piles of old newspapers in quest of grind epics. We packed up our guitars, left the amps and drums where they were, knowing we'd be back soon enough. But Stellar and I were booted from the band soon thereafter for base incompetence and inadequate respect for the Allman Brothers. Hugh took over on bass, which he played way better than me anyway. The professionals were in ascendance.

Whatcha Gonna Do?

While down the River Road at Igor's Bird Plant helicopters rolled off the line round the clock to staunch Communism in its Asian tracks, on the home front we had other fish to fry, our own internecine conflicts. Band wars were our civil strife, officially sanctioned by the powers that be: the Shelton High Key Club, St. Paul's Episcopal Church, and BSA Troop 26. Talent judges were drawn from these ranks. One—our junior high science teacher, Mr. Ritter—was seen to reach under the cafeteria table at which judges sat facing the stage to pour something into his coffee.

Band war sets were by intention short, a showcase, a forum designed to provoke participants to offer nothing but the very best they had. This necessitated a very short set indeed. Song selection was eclectic. A band, after all, wanted to impress the judges, who might also include—on top of your homeroom teacher—a parish priest or two and a local Brownie troop leader. The breadth of one's repertoire was considered a selling point. Touch all bases. Leave no Stones cover unturned. Who knows what Father Culligan digs after the folk mass, relaxing in the rectory with a goblet of communion red? I can recall Nick's Ruggerio's band following Hendrix's "The Wind Cries Mary" with a rollicking version of "1-2-3 Redlight" by the 1910 Fruitgum

Company. It doesn't seem like such a good idea in retrospect, and it didn't seem like such a good idea at the time either, if I recall correctly. But there you are. If you were playing to win, you had to appeal to the masses, mix it up. Nick had mastered Hendrix by playing *Are You Experienced?* every afternoon in his basement for months at 16 rpm. The Fruitgum Company was a picnic after that kind of stretch.

At the end of my freshman year in high school I played a band war at Sunnyside Elementary School with the Frozen Rocks, assembled exclusively to participate in the Sunnyside Band War. The Frozen Rocks gathered the competent, the barely competent, and others beneath considerations of competency under its tatty umbrella. If your body was willing and public humiliation not a problem, you were in the band. Our lead singer had never sung on a stage, or anywhere else that we could determine. I was playing an electric six-string guitar publicly for the first time, having been relieved of my bass chores by another enthusiastic neophyte. We may have had someone playing a trap set, but the instrument I best recall in our percussion section was a 20 gallon galvanized steel garbage can, turned upside down, pounded by mallets. On top of the usual suspects—the Animals' version of "C.C. Rider," and the Monkees' "Steppin' Stone"—we'd composed several original songs, including our theme song, "Be a Rock."

> *Rock rock/Be a rock*
> *Rock rock/Made from slop.*
> *Born of molten lava/Froze up in a glacier*
> *Broke out yesterday to be free*

As red-blooded American youth at the tail end of the 1960s, we were not impervious to the electric currents coursing through the air, as well as other particulate matter suspended between earth and sky, belched forth by the B.F. plant in our provincial village. Freedom was rising with the factory smoke—we could smell it through the sweet stench of burning rubber by-products. We knew instinctively that even rocks were born to be free. We simply hadn't had a vehicle and an occasion to articulate this felt sense until called on by higher powers and the Civitan Club. Our performance went to plan, or as much to plan as it could in an absence of any planning.

The other bands were displaying a brand of teenage professionalism which we were both incapable of attaining and disinterested in aspiring to. One group wore matching white turtlenecks. Two bands played the steakhouse fave "More," resuscitated by the Young Rascals, who were bigger and more influential that the Beatles and Stones combined in our neck of the woods.

Bringing the garbage can out on stage raised a few eyebrows, but we offered assurances that we had cleaned it out real good. I only played barre chords on guitar, so my hand slid up and down the neck, trying to keep pace with our tempo. I failed, but it didn't too much matter. Tim Kazo, our green lead singer, shouted loudly into his handheld microphone. Teddy Rappa—all 100 pounds of him—pounded the trash can at deafening volume in an open fake fur vest, his emaciated ribs outlined in green day-glo paint. George and I stepped to the mike to back up Tim as he shouted our other original, "Whatcha Gonna Do?"

Whatcha gonna do
If the earth breaks down
If the whole big mess

Falls to the ground
Put your working boots on
 You better leave town
Whatcha gonna do
If the earth breaks down?

It's a well-known fact that the earth is flat
Anyway/Whatcha gonna do 'bout that?
Nothin'/Nothin'/Nothin'

We scored 30 points out of 30 for musical skill with the judges, but zero out of 30 for appearance. We came in third in a field of four. I shudder to consider who under-performed us. "Whatcha Gonna Do" was later covered by local folksinger Al McKnight on a TV broadcast out of New Haven. Al was a protest singer, and ours was clearly a protest song. Whatcha gonna do? We had accidentally tapped the zeitgeist. George and I are still waiting our broadcast royalties.

The Original Joe Doy

Joe Doy had the dope and he had the girl. He had a lot of other stuff as well, and it wasn't always clear where he got it from, because one thing Joe Doy did not have was the money. The summer after ninth grade, a professional-quality movie projector appeared in Joe's basement, along with a number of reels of film. For a while we watched *The Beatles at Shea Stadium* just about every day, envying John Lennon's stylish technique of playing the Vox Continental organ with his elbows. The only other film Joe Doy had was *The Wild One*, which was less directly instructive but more subliminally influential. Two hip characters suggested we "dig the rebop, Pops" and we did. *The Wild One* proved broadly instructive in regard to general attitude. Not that we didn't see it as a period piece—the thing was fifteen years old, and to our addled sensibilities played like the *Bowery Boys on Bikes*. But it was cool in the basement, in the dark, watching a leathered-up Marlon Brando and a whack Lee Marvin. Outside, on Tuckahoe Drive, the world was hot and humid and devoid of life-size characters.

Joe Doy's Christian name was not really Joe Doy or Joseph Doy or J. Doyasevski or Declan McDoy or anything of the ilk. Joe Doy was tagged "Joe Doy" in honor of a dysfunctional, two-dimensional, tin hockey figure, and joined his youngest brother Earnickle, his sister

Ez, short for Ezmerelda—known at school as Julie—and Mr. and Mrs. Army Man, in a family living incognito under assumed names, all supplied by the middle brother George, my 3rd grade Little League bud, guitar slinger, and closet MC5 fan. No one ever gave George a handle that stuck. There are taggers, and there are the tagged.

The Original Joe Doy suffered from an inability to swivel. He was a player on a board game which was a precursor to the Foosball phenomenon which was to sweep pool tables out of neighborhood bars over the next decade. On most sweltering summer afternoons at Chez Army Man, before or after the pleasures of the umpteenth showing of the Beatles rocking Shea had been digested, shiftless members of our community could be found clustered around a four-foot long, metal hockey rink, two opponents feverishly bullying a tiny puck around the tin proscenium. The scene was always dark—light equaled heat equaled permanently drawn shades and blinds. The small room had no domestic purpose other than to house the hockey board. As with Foosball, one spun a widget connected to a rod. This spun one's player 360 degrees on command, an important offensive gesture, and provided some degree of lateral movement by which to affect defensive postures. The unfortunate contestant whose team included the Original Joe Doy, however, was stuck with a player whose capacities were purely unidirectional and rigid; the Original Joe Doy, due to irresolvable mechanical difficulties, suffered paralysis of the stick. A Bartleby of the board, he preferred not to spin. This greatly handicapped the player whose lot it was to draw the Original Joe Doy.

The similarities in character and overall usefulness to the human enterprise which George strived to establish between a three-inch high, dysfunctional tin hockey player and his older brother were readily apparent. The Original Joe Doy and Joe Doy were, in George's eyes, *doppelgangers*, figures separated at birth only by happenstance, and now joyfully reunited in the dark of the hockey board room at Chez Army Man every time Joe Doy acquiesced to engage the Original Joe Doy in combat on the iceless rink.

Doyness—once identified—flourished as an adjective, sometimes transformed by inscrutable grammatical prerogative to *doit*, as in *he's so doit, he doesn't know his ass from a hole in his shoe*. Other usage variations carried a cautionary or admonishing inflection, e.g. *don't doy out on me*, meaning: don't go rigid and useless.

Joe Doy's steady regular lost part of her first name and all of her surname in the process; she became Flore Doy. But this is really just the tip of the iceberg in regard to George's project, which was to rename all of God's creatures to his liking and their true nature. Brother Earnickel was early on called Ape-er-Nackel. The referent, beyond its obvious connection with simian qualities so evident in most younger brothers, is tough to source. Ape-er-Nackel eventually morphed into Earn-a-Nickel, as Steve (birth name) would do just about anything for any amount of money, vs. George, who would do just about nothing for any reason whatsoever. Earn-a-Nickel proved to have one too many syllables to roll off the tongue, and quickly enough transformed to Earnickel. As with *doy*, Earnickel soon acquired broad application outside the Army household. It came to denote any pre-adolescent male approximately three years younger than we were. As in, *I saw a bunch of Earnickels sharing a Camel, heading down to the Pickerel Pond with a soggy Playboy*.

Army Man had never been in any army I was aware of. I believe he acquired his handle simply because he occasionally made what seemed to me to be fairly reasonable fatherly demands of his charges, along the lines of "please don't light anything in the basement on fire, George," and made them in the not altogether dulcet tones of an individual who had grown up in the Bronx. Army Lady was of an even milder disposition, seemingly un-phased by any variety of havoc her progeny were facilitating. Army Man and Army Lady were two reasons we spent so much time at Army Headquarters. They were the poster parents of mellow.

A low-level, constant chaos and a sense of permanent open house permeated Army Headquarters. Someone was usually slouching on an Easy Boy in the living room as you entered, playing an unplugged or thoroughly gutted electric guitar. If you were an Earnickel, you approached the home with caution, as you were likely to serve as a live target for someone shooting a pellet gun out George's bedroom window. It was the first home I ate in where pets had free-range privileges on the dinner table. Proper etiquette demanded holding the fork in your right hand while batting the cat with your left.

Chez Army pulled out what little stops remained for high Holy Days. It was where the *hoi polloi* met before staggering down to midnight mass on Christmas Eve. I would enter the packed home to find Army Man the central attraction, reclining in his Easy Boy with a leather World War II flier's helmet on his head, little round Jack Casady shades shielding him from scrutiny, a half gallon of vodka in hand. Army Man in the world was a card-carrying adult—an engineer of some sort for GE. He didn't play those cards at home.

Mr. Maher! Merry Christmas!
Santa?
Yes, Mr. Maher.
Don't EVER call me Mr. Maher.
Sure, Mr Maher. I mean, Army Man.

Dominus vobiscum, Army Man. For a while, we thought if we could rename the world, memorize the Beatles' moves at Shea Stadium, and dig the rebop, we could own some of that world. Then the bank repossessed the projector.

Papa's Got a Brand New Thumb Cymbal

The Frozen Rocks, unfortunately, were a one-off. There was limited capacity in our neck of the woods for a combo driven by a mallet-beaten, galvanized garbage can, espousing flat-world sentiments. Stellar and I had been banished from Hugh's basement. I was learning to strum tunes on the Greco, but I didn't have the patience or manual dexterity for learning licks and practicing scales.

I'd sit next to Robbie in his dark basement bedroom, on the edge of his bed, listening to James Brown's song "Licking Stick." It's got that syncopated, hammered-off suspension chord, the signature rhythm and riff of James Brown's hits of the late-60s. Robbie's figured this out. He's playing his unplugged Gibson SG, trying to teach me the riff. Or simply displaying his chops, as the likelihood of me being able to replicate a guitar riff off a James Brown record was slim to none. We were a long way from super bad. Just two white boys, 14 and 15 years old, trying to swallow some funk.

But Robbie was really trying to digest the funk—I was slipping into a consumer role. I was a huge fan, but I couldn't see clearly to a place in a band which demanded such finesse. I should have known I wasn't going to play well with the other kids when I bought The Incredible String Band's *The Hangman's Beautiful Daughter* in downtown Bridgeport shortly after its release during my freshman year of high school. The Incredible String Band was as far from James Brown as Pluto is from the sun—it is barely in the same planetary system. It's difficult to reconstruct the logic behind my purchase. An impulse buy? Probably not in a strict sense—I was a money manager without much to manage, and I didn't indulge myself very frequently. Maybe there'd been some blurb in the Sunday *NY Times*, which I'd peruse like a Martian trying to understand the denizens of Earth from my far outpost. I'd yet to cast eyes on a *Rolling Stone*, as the head shop under the railroad tracks down by UB had yet to open, depriving us for another year of prism-lensed pink shades. In any case, I bought the Incredible String Band LP, headed over to the bus station, took the bus out to the end of the line in Stratford and hitch-hiked the remaining miles home, eager to hear what I'd gotten myself into.

Amoebas are very sm—all

I soon learned. The cover depicted a build-your-own-gypsy family with principals Mike Heron and Robin Williamson at the center. The weirdly resonating stringed instruments of obscure national origin were right up my alley. Heron's and Williamson's voices were by turns chipper, stoned, and wobbly, as were their lyrics:

OOOhhh/Next week a monkey is coming to stay.
Really? Can I come too? I promise not to shit on the floor.

The melodies tangled sitar and mandolin around creaking, harmonium-driven Protestant hymns. The Incredible String Band was a hard sell to my old bandmates and town buds, plugged in as they were to *Electric Mud* and *Blodwyn Pig*. They humored my interest in the thumb cymbal set as a sort of vitamin deficiency, akin to my tendencies towards the MC5. Perhaps I'd come around, if only I could be exposed daily to Jeff Beck's *Truth*. My new desire to take up the mandolin alienated me from my Allman brothers, who had difficulty getting beyond the mandolin's association with elderly *bocce* ball aficionados.

The sound of the mandolin piqued my curiosity. I was in my sophomore year before I took the dive. Mandolins tinkered in the background of stuff I was listening to beyond the off-keel Incredible String Band—the Byrd's *Sweetheart of the Rodeo*, for instance. Then *Let It Bleed* came out, and guess what's on side A, track 2—Ry Cooder's mandolin. I kept my lookout, and when Cooder's first solo LP was released, I was first in line. Mind you—I had no idea whatsoever of the existence of bluegrass music or Bill Monroe (let alone my future role model—Buzz Buzby). What I was listening to came from the narrow if rich vein of playing derived from country blues and Memphis jug band music, via Cooder. Part of my thinking was that I preferred being the best (if only) mandolinist among my peers rather than the sixth best guitarist in a room with five other friends.

So as my peer's tastes moved away from bash-it-out garage rock toward more sophisticated expressions of musical prowess, I became something of a closeted, self-educated folky. Mostly self-educated. Up in the hills of our town where a few dairy farms hung on, a small store stood off a dirt parking lot on Route 110. The store's hand-painted marquee read: BAIT and MUSICAL INSTRUMENTS. I had noticed this place a few years ago, passing it on the Boy Scout hike where I both learned to smoke cigarettes and gave up the habit on the same day. I stopped in on my bike one day as I was short of guitar picks and I couldn't conjure a closer place where I could find picks. I didn't need any bait that day, but I wouldn't have been disappointed. The small room was neatly divided—fishing poles, lures, packages of hooks to one side, a few guitars on stands and a saxophone and trumpet on the wall to the other. The small front counter was similarly bifurcated, with a plastic jar of picks on one side.

"How much are the picks?" I asked.

"A quarter," he burped.

I'm not speaking figuratively. He burped this at me.

"Five for a dollar," he added, deeply froggy.

I was looking at this old fellow without responding, my mouth no doubt hanging open. I imagine he was used to this. He pointed to his neck, where I now detected a small, healed up incision, then with two fingers to his mouth, pantomimed smoking.

"Don't—get— started," he burped, leveling a steady gaze at me.

I offered him a buck, took five picks, and turned to his inventory, wandering through the wares to collect myself.

I wanted to indicate to him that I'd somewhat accomplished this, and went back to the register.

"What are those metal things?" I asked, pointing to a smaller plastic container on the counter, next to the picks.

"Slides," he said, and was already out from behind the counter. He grabbed one of the guitars off its stand and sat down on the only chair in the room. He put the guitar across his lap and began to strum. Then he applied the solid, bullet-shaped bar to the strings at the fifth fret, wiggling the thing down to the third fret before returning to the open strumming, which sounded like a chord made without any fretting.

"Leon McAuliffe," he said, smiling up at me.

In a moment I'd learned the name of Bob Wills and the Texas Playboys steel guitarist and how Keith Richard's made all that whining noise on *Beggar's Banquet*.

My mother—the nurse—had to explain to me later how laryngeal cancer can obliterate one's voice box, and how a tracheostomy can sometimes provide an alternative option to using your voice box to speak. Rough stuff. If I hadn't already given up smoking after one afternoon, that might have done it for me. Before I'd left, I'd asked Sam—the bait shop steel player—if he'd give me a lesson on playing as he did. I'd taken a few bass guitar lessons at Banko's at one time, but I mostly struggled through this stuff myself. I ended up taking two lessons with Sam in the back room of his shop. He showed me how to hold the guitar on my lap, manipulate the solid steel slide, and tune the guitar up to an open G or D chord. It sounded cool as hell, but once home, I realized I had enough trouble getting the Greco into standard tuning. After breaking a few strings as I retuned the guitar, I gave up that project for the time being, but Sam planted a seed. Leon McAuliffe, huh? And who the hell's Bob Wills?

As You'll Ever Be

I was in that weird age vortex where pop music was so central to my daily life but so hard to get out and see in its natural habitat. It was a CYO church group that took me to see the Grateful Dead at Yale Bowl in eighth grade—with openers Gary Puckett and the Union Gap. There's got to be a strange Holiday Inn story there, no? School dances were kind of corny and far too well-lit, but I do recall seeing fabulous Al Anderson and the Wild Weeds nail a killer version of "I Am the Walrus" at St. Joe's High School. The more typical bands that played at our school dances were a barometer of how far we lagged on the national hip-o-meter. They were usually seven or eight pieces, a three-man horn section, enormous Hammond organ which required a crane to get it on stage, a front man with his hair slicked back, pointed cockroach-impaling pimp shoes, tight slacks of 100% synthetic material purchased at Chess King in the Trumbull Mall, a vest thrown in to frame a shirt, purple or pink, with ruffles.

The 60s took a long time arriving in our neck of the woods—the decade was just about tapped out on the clock when they arrived. I can recall listening to *Workingman's Dead* with Chuck and Robbie, sleeping over at Robbie's grandmother's river-front cottage down by the Housatonic, standing in our underwear about three feet from a moving freight train, high on mild weed and four Rheingold small boys shared between the three of us. The 60's arrived on that freight train headed up the Valley, I think. Our peers bifurcated now into two groups: the heads and everyone else. Having identified as musicians for several years, and been identified by our peers as musicians, it was immediately assumed we used drugs, and sooner or later, that assumption proved correct. It was pretty innocuous stuff in retrospect, mostly marijuana and the occasional chunk of hash, but the cultural divide between users and non-users was a chasm, and the ramifications of being caught in *flagrante delicto* by John Law were not inconsequential.

We were just as much booze hounds as drug offenders, drinking whatever we could score illegally or steal from family members. Surreptitious consumption and the random nature of supply proved a recipe for sloppy drunk. If we had it, we drank it, quick. The results were somewhat predictable.

For instance: we'd arrived at a point where some of us could drive, and our buddies the Pigpen Blues Band were playing at a chicken coop converted into a teen center in Newtown, so several of us decided it would be a styling thing to do to go surprise them at this far-flung gig fifteen miles from home. In our town they'd turned the U.S. Army's Nike missile site into the teen center. I guess we didn't have a Superfund site full of toxic waste available, so the town fathers figured we could suffer nuclear bomb dust.

I'd briefly been in a 9th grade band with Howard E., a.k.a. Pigpen, Hendrix acolyte Nick, and drummer Mucho, a delicate youth whose real expertise in this world was tying exquisite fishing flies. Nick's backyard 12 x 18 bungalow was at the time action central for all young musicians with time on their hands, which meant all of us. The clubhouse was fitted with an irregularly performing stereo, its turntable now randomly slowing to the 16 rpm's necessary for interpreting Hendrix's fingerwork. Let me tell you—Ron Bushy's interminable drum solo on "In-A-Gadda-Da-Vida" does not get better played at 16 rpm. It is the aural equivalent of drowning in a tar pit.

For reasons that completely escape me, anyone walking into Nick's bungalow was immediately in danger of receiving a wedgie for breaching one inarticulate rule of protocol or another. Wedgies derived from a form of latently homoerotic Sumo wrestling. The loser of this athletic exercise frequently found the back of his tighty whities up around his neck while still wearing the same. One could go from a baritone to a soprano in seconds. Howard was too large and formidable to suffer this treatment and Chuck took the precaution of never wearing underwear to Nick's. At one point Mucho pleaded that he was down to his last pair of underwear. Howard could sing for real and Nick was no slouch on guitar, but with Mucho and I as rhythm section we demonstrated something short of Zep-power as a quartet.

We had a hard time just finding this gig that the Pigpens were playing in the boonies. And to add insult to the injury of burning a dollar of gas to get there, the authorities were requiring two dollars at the door. My more sheep-like companions paid up, but Stir Dudko and I were having none of that fudge, and we resolutely circled the old chicken house looking for an open window.

The place was configured something like a concrete missile silo lying on its side—long and narrow, with few windows. When we got to the rear of the building, a steel garage door stretched almost the length of the room. I peered through the door's glass panes and could see the Pigpens directly in front of us, their backs to the door, rocking a Rick Derringer tune to the small, bell-bottomed crowd in front of them. No need to enter upside down through an open window—just walk right in, sit right down, baby let your mind roll on. Look at these suckers. Two dollars for a handstamp, when they all could have been backdoor men, like us. With a burst of adrenaline and a heave, I threw open the garage door.

The electric tumult came to an immediate halt. My buddy Dana, whom I'd known since 2nd grade, was on drums. He kept beating the kit for another bar, then he stopped too. Everyone in the band began peering frantically in every direction, attempting to identify the source of *coitus interruptus*. Stir adroitly flattened himself behind an amp. The fact that I had suddenly appeared behind Dude, standing in front of an open three-car garage door, slack-jawed, deer-in-the-headlights, the nasty November evening invading what had just a second before been a warm rock and roll hootchy cocoon of humming hormones did not serve to explain anything. I spied a men's room to my immediate left. Having dislocated the band's master electric cord from its socket in one swell foop, I retired to a bathroom stall, locked the door, and hopped up on a toilet seat in my snowy work boots, crouching there to wait out this minor inconvenience, listening to the next ten minutes of piss room chatter about the asshole who unplugged us all.

Ring Ring Goes the Bell

I was attending a Catholic boys high school. This was just one reason why this variety of misadventure was an almost exclusively same-sex exercise—our rigorous daily academic routine offered zero opportunity for interaction with the fair sex, and hence, no forum in which to develop the social skills handy for the rare occasions when this interaction might occur. Dancing with the opposite sex—such a prime feature of the St. Paul's dances of our junior high years—had fallen out of favor, replaced by a passive audience spectating a musical "performance."

But our school—drawing as it did from communities scattered across a county—was a bouillabaisse of bad behavior developed in our varied K-8 schools. Stated among OBJECTIVES OF YOUR SCHOOL as articulated in our 1969-1970 *Student Handbook* was that a four year apprenticeship would leave us "well on the way to the finished product of the perfect Christian gentleman, well prepared to make this earth a better place for living." I appreciate in retrospect that the Jesuits focused on terrestrial vs. celestial goals, but they had their work cut out for themselves nonetheless. Our student body featured an all-star team of reprobates, and reached something of a pinnacle in that regard in my class year. The class two years ahead of us had twelve Merit Scholar finalists. Our class had none. In that older class of achievers, there was fierce animosity between the Vietnam War-protesting, Earth Day-supporting hipsters and the football-playing preppies. In our class, the heads and jocks hung together, brothers in dissipation. When the public high school in my town teetered on the brink of losing accreditation after our sophomore year, three of my guitar-toting chums transferred into our student body. The school dropped its short hair-only dress code. One could now wear a turtleneck in place of a tie, just like Hugh Hefner. Things were clearly going to hell.

For some reason my parents decided around this time that it was alright to stay with one of my high school friends one Friday night and grab a train to NYC to see a show at the Fillmore East. I think this was based on the mistaken impression they held that consorting with anyone beyond my now long-haired hometown gang was a preferable option. Long hair had all sorts of signifying capacity in the weird teenage micro-moment I inhabited, and to my parents (my dad—the ex-Marine, Parris Island-trained), none of it was good. Cave N. had a Wally Haskell-like capacity to charm parents, but he ran with a neighbor, Face, whose claim to fame was a backyard bomb shelter with an apocalypse-appropriate supply of Seconals. Cave N.'s mom drove us down to the train station and we grabbed an express to Grand Central, rolled into its cavernous and bustling great hall, and figured out how we'd get downtown. I'd never been in a New York subway car before. I goaded Cave. N. into asking the conductor where the bar car was. He didn't look much older than us, awkward in his blue uniform MTA uniform and cap.

"*Bar* car?"

"Yeah," Cave N. insisted earnestly. "The bar car."

"Bar car? Ain't no *bar* car."

The young conductor screwed his face into a combination of bewilderment and disgust as Cave N. walked back to our seats.

We got off at Astor Place, near Cooper Union, and worked to orient ourselves above ground. We walked past the Electric Circus. The whole neighborhood seemed like a circus to me—a carnival. Urban odors permeated the air—a mix of human body scent, diesel fumes, fried food, and decaying plant and animal matter. We found the Fillmore East, paid our $4.50 each for balcony tickets, and took in the Nice, with Keith Emerson's enormous wall of keyboards, and the Byrds—with no one but Roger McGuinn left from the original band of five years ago. A weird bill, for sure.

Fillmore East bills continued with these eclectic matches and we caught a few of them. Mott the Hoople—with Sha-Na-Na? Moby Grape and B.B. King. Perhaps the weirdest and best bargain for our money was the night we caught Miles Davis opening for the Steve Miller Band and Neil Young and Crazy Horse. It was Miller and Young, of course, who attracted our febrile teenage sensibilities and motivated us to upgrade to $6.50 floor seats, but it was Davis who took us back to school. Davis's band was like a future Jazz Hall of Fame gathering: Wayne Shorter, Dave Holland, Chick Corea, Jack DeJohnette, Airto Moreira. *Bitches Brew* would be released the following month. The music was dense, consuming, confusing. Davis played sparingly himself, punctuating pieces with odd shrieks from his trumpet, or playing quietly when things calmed down a bit, which was not often. Poor Steve Miller had to follow this with a stripped down trio. We'd been big fans of his first two albums, when he shared singing and songwriting with Boz Scaggs. This wasn't that band, and even we could feel his pain. Young rose to the challenge of the occasion and blasted out of the tube with "Everybody Knows This Is Nowhere," Danny Whitten on second guitar and second vocals, angelic background voices from the rest of Crazy Horse. Still, ten minutes into his circuitous solo on "Cowgirl in the Sand" it was clear who'd won this cutting contest.

We'd retreat to our home-ground after forays like this and scratch our heads. At least I would. It was maybe eighty miles as the crow flies from our homes to the Lower East Side, but we might as well have crossed an ocean to get there. I couldn't in the farthest corner of my skull imagine carrying the horn bag or guitar case of these Goliaths. The experience drove me further into my acoustic guitar and mandolin noodling. I transposed Robert Johnson's "Four 'til Late" to mandolin. It was a pinnacle achievement for me, but there was no way I was going to play it in public, let alone sing a Robert Johnson lyric in front of other people. My consciousness had moved a step beyond earnest renditions of "House of the Rising Sun," but it was a bit of an endgame. I was clearly not Eric Clapton—have never been mistaken for him—nor was I a young black man from the Mississippi Delta in the 1930s. So who was I? Anonymous back-up musician would have been nice, but the opportunity did not present itself.

It's 1969 (in 1972), OK?

I grabbed the Stooges first album down at Woolworth's one day after my shift washing dishes at Friendly's Ice Cream. I must have read something about it which appealed to me—no one I knew had an inkling of who the Stooges were, nor would they have willingly listened for more than half a minute after being exposed to "1969."

It's 1969 OK?/All across the USA
Another day for me and you/Another day with nothing to do

I—on the other hand—found the Stooges kind of thrilling. I was getting bookish at some level. Not that I hadn't always read a lot once I discovered the Hardy Boys in 4th grade. But I bought *On the Road* the month after Kerouac died, along with Lenny Bruce's *How to Talk Dirty and Influence People* and Chuang Tzu's *Genius of the Absurd*. We were reading Dostoyevsky's *Notes From the Underground*, Camus's *The Stranger*, and Nietzsche's *Twilight of the Idols*—in my required theology class. But another part of me longed for the elemental stupidity of "Louie Louie." I missed the Kingsmen. The Stooges plugged me back into that current. It was a guilty pleasure, for sure. My friends humored me. They were kind, mostly, and after the Incredible String Band, they realized my tastes were a bit skew.

Meanwhile, several close buds were moving on by staying put. Though our high school was ostensibly training each of us for college, by senior year Robbie and Hugh decided to stick at home with their almost full-time gigs as musicians. The drinking age was dropping to 18 and the bar band trade was flourishing. Robbie and Hugh weren't playing the hits. Robbie's band dug deep into obscure album cuts from Albert King and Jesse Ed Davis, and brought them to life with sharp, soulful execution. Hugh was playing something suspiciously close to jazz. But the one thing that wasn't really happening on our front was songwriting. That—of course—was how one was going to get a recording contract and a record made. But none of us thought that through. Songwriting comes later, right? It's the natural progression of skilled musicians. You applied talent and incessant woodshedding until you were worthy enough to write a song. *Whatcha gonna to do if the earth breaks down?* Play another Johnny Winter song, apparently.

The one band to break out of our rusting industrial blot on the map was Steam. *Na-na-na-na/Na-na-na-na/Hey hey-ah/Goodbye.* This perennial baseball stadium chant encapsulated a sensibility permeating our backwater. See you later, alligator. The chorus is a nursery rhyme, of course, and the song's a one-off recording by a bunch of locals goofing in the studio, tape rolling by accident probably. Is this not how true classic rock and roll is recorded? Screaming Jay Hawkins was so drunk he couldn't even remember recording "I Put a Spell on You."

But listen up next time your car radio scan lands on the oldies station. Be patient—you won't have to wait long for some Steam. The vocal has surprising soul. The vibes, an idea lifted from Motown productions, lubricate the enterprise like a shot of WD-40. The gang vocals are a primordial chorus. The fade's artful, like listening to the St. Augustine band march off down St. Charles Avenue on Mardi Gras morning. Steam—the stuff you let off when you're boiling inside, blown away in the dirty wind.

During spring break in senior year, a half dozen of us drove down to a small community north of Boone, NC where a local Catholic priest was engaged in community outreach projects. We would work with two families while there for a week, flooring a cabin in one case and replacing the roof shingles of a small house in town. We slept in the basement of the church, with one of our school's Jesuit teachers, Father Dan, as our chaperone. I'd tried to smuggle along a fifth of vodka in a wine bota, but it ruptured in my sleeping bag somewhere in the Shenandoah Valley.

"What's that smell," Father Dan inquired.

"I think I broke my bottle of aftershave, father," our driver Jared suggested.

We were back in the hills for sure. One night we caught a film at the movie theatre in town, a sci-fi feature in which a co-ed team of astronauts on the moon were forced to disrobe in their moon rover due to the extreme temperatures. Patrons actually threw rotten vegetables at the screen. I bought a worn $15 Kay electric guitar at a pawn shop in town at lunch one day. We were roofing that day, and by the end of the day my hands were so covered with roofing tar that I was effectively down to two functioning fingers on each hand. The family whose house we were working on generously insisted we share dinner with them and we scraped our hands as clean as we could with turpentine and rags. After dinner, Jared mentioned my purchase of the Kay at lunch. Oh—play us a song, please.

I was stunned. I had no problem joining in on the choruses of "Be a Rock" at the Sunnyside Band War, but this was different altogether. A solo performance, just me, singing?

I was backed into a corner, at a loss as to what to do or play, but even more fearful of appearing rude. I reluctantly picked up the Kay, looked down to its strings, and broke into the riff of Elvis's "Mystery Train." The Kay—an unplugged electric—was none too loud, but I beat the strings and dove into my best imitation of the King.

The family loved it. They were being kind, of course. The Kay's neck was now greased with turpentine and spotted with roofing tar.

School ended. The war in Viet Nam, which had shadowed our adolescence and incited our sense that the world was at heart insane, was winding down. Unlike townies just a year or two older, none of us felt an imminent fear of the draft. Every member of our undistinguished high school class somehow graduated. I had not been a great student, but I was a good test-taker. I worked at my family's business as a plumber's assistant, saving money before wandering off toward college. I took a road trip up to the Canadian Maritime provinces with my Friendly's boss Rocky, a year older than me. Rocky was staying in town, planning his marriage. We listened to Joni Mitchell's *Blue* constantly on that road trip, a weird soundtrack for two bachelor boys. Stayed in a 18th century prison converted into a hostel run by a mescaline-gobbling staff in Quebec City, slept on the floor in a roomful of real bums for a buck a night in St John's, attended a provincial street fair way out east in Sydney, Nova Scotia, the edge of the continent, feeling as if we'd skipped over the ocean to Glasgow.

I had a dream a few weeks before leaving for school. *It's a well-known fact that the earth is flat.* But it took me some time to walk to the edge. There's a railing at the lip, not too high, kind of like the railing they used to have at the top of the Empire State Building back in the 40s, which my father's friend Flynn used to sit on, legs over the edge. I came up to the railing and leaned tentatively over: I'm no Flynn. Bending myself in half, I could just see enough of the other side of the earth to determine that it is all black and concentrically grooved—our flat earth has a B-side. Far in the distance, I could just make out the yellow and white zebra-striped label of London Records. The flip side of the earth is the Rolling Stones' "Time Is On My Side." Tiny human figures walked upside down, stuck to the grooves in their gravity boots. That—I said to myself—is where I want to be.

ACT II

Mandolin Town

I left home to attend college in the nation's capital. I would put childish things behind me and begin the painful, unfamiliar motions of becoming an adult and a functional, contributing member of civil society.

Hedging my bets, I brought a Gibson J-200 acoustic, the Kay electric, a hollow-body, cherry red Gibson EB-2 bass, and my Harmony mandolin. Most of these instruments were stolen, broken in half, or bartered for beer money in the next two years. My intentions were benign, but in retrospect this was an awful lot of distraction from anything academic.

Despite ample paraphernalia, I did not actively pursue a public life as a musician. Notions of one day being as big as the Kingsmen were shelved as I applied half my ass to school. But I soon discovered the plethora of record stores in the big city, and the other half began to wander. I harangued my hall mates with dissertations on and demonstrations of the sublime pleasures of Michael Hurley and the Bonzo Dog Band, two of my high school sweethearts, and combed the vinyl racks for new treasure. Within the course of my first year in D.C. I purchased Gram Parsons' *GP*, Big Star's *Radio City*, and Richard Thompson's initial solo album, *Henry the Human Fly*. I'd dug the

Sandy Denny-era Fairport Convention and was taken by Thompson's dada-esque posture on the cover. These three albums combined represented my lodestar: country (vs. country-rock), Beatle-esque pop with a nasty streak, and twisted Celtic folk. But look to the Billboard Top 100 charts of the early 1970s. Number 1 in 1973: "Tie a Yellow Ribbon Round the Ole Oak Tree." My predilections did not bode well for reconciliation down the road with mainstream American pop n' roll.

My political antennae were askew as well. I marched with the throng down Pennsylvania Avenue the day of Nixon's second inauguration, but veered off at 18th Street and walked up to a modest second story studio for my guitar lesson. I was trying to learn chords which were not on the first two pages of the Mel Bay primer. While this instruction did not include the option of buying a Chinese take-out box of earthworms on completion, after four lessons I could play reasonable facsimiles of augmented chords and thus terminated my apprenticeship. That was the extent of my formal training on stringed instruments. I have long owed my amateur status and hard-earned ineptitude to an inability to take sensible direction or advice.

Though I had no idea on arrival, D.C. was a mandolin town—the bluegrass capital of America. I was a neophyte, but my next door neighbor Bob Perilla fixed that. Bob was Maryland-Italian hillbilly gentry. His grandfather had run with H.L. Mencken in Baltimore, his father healed the sick at Johns Hopkins Hospital, and like me, Bob had been incarcerated by the Jesuits during his high school years. But Bob grew up on a farm out in Howard County, and he just couldn't wipe the shit off his boots. In fact, he never tried—Bob admired the smell and feel of shit on his boots and the wide swath of sidewalk it afforded his substantial defensive lineman frame on the cobbled streets of Georgetown, where we'd by-pass the rock clubs and find ourselves among a dozen customers in an M Street bar listening to a tubercular middle-aged man with a buzz cut sitting on a wooden stool under a single light, playing a Fender Telecaster, singing antique country music.

Ry Cooder and Chris Hillman were the only mandolinists I'd ever heard on record. It was Bob who introduced me to the sublime joys of Buzz Busby, who was to the mandolin what Jerry Lee Lewis was to the piano, and like Jerry, a Louisiana transplant grown kudzu-wild. Years later, Bob claimed that Busby, who lived around D.C. for the better part of his adult life, had a day job as an elementary school principal. Really? Busby's 1970 LP with Leon Morris—*Honkytonk Bluegrass*—began to regularly rotate on my turntable.

The Buddy System

Joe Doy's bands were always on the verge of the Big Break. First, the Lavender Blue, runaway victor of the Shelton High band war during ninth grade. We thought vocalist Harrison Buster (real name!) would be the next soul superstar, any minute now. His voice was like something off a record and he looked like Sam Cooke's little brother. He must have been at least a junior in high school. Joe Doy's battery mate, bassist Dave Hull, was also a germinal rockstah. Skinny? To the extreme. Hair? Much. Chops? Ditto. We were dirt beneath the heels of these giants.

But even in the land of giants, there are the truly gigantic. Bigger men—such was Buddy Miles. Hardly even done with high school, Dave and his running partner Charlie Karp got scarfed up by Miles. Who knows the real story? Certainly not me, so here it goes. Miles had been drummer in the Electric Flag, a multi-racial horn-driven supergroup littered with colorful and difficult personalities. By May 1969 he was touring with his own aggregation, the Buddy Miles Express, and found himself on stage in Westport at Staples, the public high school in a town with close to the highest per capita income in the country. In short, the home of the blues. In New York City in December 1969, rehearsing with Jimi Hendrix's Band of Gypsies trio, Buddy booked a second gig at Staples. But when Buddy took the stage, the large ensemble Express had been stripped down to a trio—Buddy on drums and local lights Dave and Charlie Karp on bass and guitar.

Buddy had taken a shine to Dave and Charlie and shortly into the new year invited them to L.A. They were soon Angelenos, still teenagers, living off oranges they stole from neighbors' trees in the midnight hour. I believe Joe Doy made the move with them, but never cracked the band line-up. Dave and Charlie were soon on the road with the full-strength Express, by-passing senior year on a world tour.

Buddy was larger than life to us, seminal, the Ur-Drummer. Companion and battery mate of Hendrix in his earthiest incarnation would have been enough. But as substantial as Buddy's musical presence proved to be, the stories surrounding Buddy are what spoke to us. They represented an essence of *pura vida* which cannot be reduced to an exhibit in the Rock and Roll Hall of Fame. What would be exhibited? The iron skillet with which Joey Wirsing, neighbor of George and Joe Doy, older brother of Bird Snot, and ultimately road manager of the Buddy Miles Express, bopped his rambunctious employer over the head one coke-addled morning? The closet of XXL Nudie suits Buddy absconded with from the renowned Hollywood clothier to the stars? The towering stack of hotel bills from which Buddy ran. The empty 15-piece KFC bucket which Buddy reduced to bones on the way to a Thanksgiving dinner at Nick Gravenites's place in Marin? The pink panties slipped from one of Hefner's harem, worn as a hairnet to his ever expanding Afro shortly after his *Playboy After Dark* gig?

By 1972, Dave and Charlie had fled Buddy's galley, executed a brief detour to Arthur Lee's post-Love unit, then reunited in CT with Joe Doy as White Chocolate. During my first semester of college in D.C. I had the honor of warehousing Joe Doy in the hammock hanging wall-to-wall in my dorm room during a weekend club gig White Chocolate had opening for Rory Gallagher's Taste. Roommate Rick Baitz and I scored a place on the guest list and took in the smoky affair. At the end of a blurry day and night, Joe Doy offered me Buddy's long-distance calling card number. Use it in the spirit of Buddy, he suggested.

Phone calls used to cost real money, of which we were chronically short. I was soon in almost daily touch with my girlfriend Kathleen back home. Rick's family lived in South Africa, and they became recipients of lengthy calls from their wayward boy back in the States. We were generous with Buddy's largesse. Our dorm floor's one pay phone stood outside our room—anyone at a loss for a few spare quarters to call home soon understood to come knocking at our door. By the time Bell South caught up with us, the 4th floor of Healy Hall was several thousand dollars into Buddy's wallet. We pled ignorance to the lions-share of charges, though Rick couldn't shake the circumstantial evidence linking him to hundreds of dollars of calls to the Southern Hemisphere. I plead nolo to calls to a certain number in Connecticut. We paid our share and learned our lesson: drop the dime or cop to the crime. There are things only Buddy can get away with.

Four years later I was in a casual conversation with a new friend in San Francisco, a life-long resident of Marin County who had grown up a cowboy there, when that was still possible. For whatever reason, the conversation rolled around to Buddy—I think John had known a horn player in the Express. "You know," John said, "for the longest time, we used this calling card number which _____ had given us." Buddy's tender mercies were spread o'er the world.

Unstrung

Bob and I played a couple of college coffee house gigs, terrifying from my perspective, laid out for scrutiny in this low decibel setting in a way I never was playing "Louie Louie" or self-penned, band war inanities. Stage fright, however, was nothing which a fifth of Rebel Yell bourbon prior to show time couldn't fix. Rebel Yell bourbon created, exacerbated, and temporarily ameliorated most of my dilemmas at this point in time. I stayed in town that summer and Bob and I began rehearsing with several of his high school chums as the Unstrung Heroes. Our vision—fuzzy at best—outreached our grasp, and the band never made it out of the basement. My mandolin technique could best have been described as garageabilly. I was trying to transpose the spirit of Chuck Berry's guitar playing to soloing on the mandolin, without much success, but with much shredding of strings as I pounded the frets. Our experiment disintegrated around the time my mandolin disappeared from the backseat of a bandmate's old convertible.

I was making my rent working 4pm to 2am every Friday and Saturday night bussing tables at the Bayou, a rock and roll toilet on K Street which gained some notoriety in years after my departure. At the time it featured the usual horrible early 70s cover bands. The weekend nights would begin with our restocking the beer bins, reserving the coldest bottles from the bottom of the bin for our own refreshment.

We'd depart the Bayou after closing on Saturday with a huge batch of pre-mixed cocktails appropriated from the walk-in freezer. That's when our weekend really began. Needless to say, this practice was a lousy sync with study habits. I also put in some time washing dishes at the Apple Pie on M Street, where house band the Dubonnettes served as D.C.'s answer to the New York Dolls. Years later Dubonnettes guitarist Mike Stern swerved hard virtuoso, including a stint as Miles Davis's guitarist. Most of my Apple Pie colleagues spent their entire Apple Pie paycheck in the Apple Pie—a sort of conveniently indentured servitude. We owed our soul to the company store. I would sometimes come in for a lunch shift at 11am to find two people present, the owner—sleeping on the bar—and Nils Lofgren, playing endless rounds of Pong, an early video game requiring prehensile manipulation of a joystick and minimal mental concentration. Pong was trance inducing and addictive.

The town had lots of other opportunities designed to thwart academic pursuits—Emmylou Harris at the Cellar Door, Danny Gatton at our neighborhood bar, Rambling Jack Elliot and Charles Mingus and Pharoah Saunders at clubs near Dupont Circle. Leo Kottke played a small hall just off campus while I was still nominally in school. I had a real appetite for Kottke's 12-string slide and 6-string guitar ruminations. As someone who really didn't see himself as a lead singer, his early instrumental albums spoke to me. But by the time I went looking for a ticket, his show had sold out. The night of the show I circled the hall, an old church. No garage doors to lift. It was snowing. I pulled myself up a gutter pipe to a roof next to the hall. An open second story window appeared to be airing out the men's room. Pulling myself up to the window sill, I saw two fellows at urinals with their backs to me. It was quite a drop from the window sill to the floor, but the only way in was upside down. Fortunately, there was a radiator directly under the window to break my fall. Now or not—over and down. I scalded my palms on the radiator, but flipped to the checkerboard tile floor. One of the pissers turned to me. "Music should be free" I flatly stated, pushing through the doors of the loo. Ah—youth. It was a sentiment I'd come to reconsider down the line, when I was on the other side of this transaction. Kottke was just taking the stage and I found a seat in an aisle, my hands burning.

As I turned 20, I took a gig waiting tables downtown at the Old Ebbitt Grill on F street, three blocks from the White House. This was the old Old Ebbitt, not the current posh version—about as wide as a railway car and smelling of home-made fries. On my first shift, a slow Sunday afternoon, I spilled red wine on Burl Ives and didn't get fired. During the week, I got the shittiest wait station, as the newest and youngest waiter on staff and a wine spiller to boot, right down next to the flaming kitchen. This was where Carl Bernstein set up camp, all the way to the back, out of sight. It was the summer of 1974, and Nixon was hanging by a string of dental floss. Vultures hovered over the Potomac. Hunter S. Thompson would come into the Ebbitt occasionally. He was by far the best of the Hunter S. Thompson imitators, right down to the cigarette holder.

Around this time I dropped the pretense of college enrollment.

Then after a fall season of work, I was cut loose from the Ebbitt. Though the Unstrung Heroes had unspooled, I continued to imagine myself a mandolinist—I spent most of my savings on an ancient Gibson A-model mandolin at Mandolin Brothers in Staten Island. Our apartment lease ending, I hatched a plan to migrate south.

I bought a ticket on Amtrak to Jacksonville out of Union Station on the first of the year. Jacksonville was as far into Florida as my limited resources could bear. I left mid-afternoon and slept in my seat that night, waking up to spring outside the window. In Savannah I stepped out onto the station platform to take in the blossoming flowers and warm sun. Now I understood why everyone's grandparents fled New England come January. I disembarked in Jacksonville and began hitching south, pink flamingos in the ditches and swamped fields next to the Interstate entrance. The year before I'd hitched from Wisconsin to Connecticut the day after a Midwestern blizzard with $1.25 in my pocket—this was like a vacation by comparison. Was it a vacation? Not really, in my mind. But I was headed to Fort Lauderdale, then hopefully on to Key West, with few plans beyond reaching the end of the road.

Getting to the end of the road can be a challenge. I had a long ride down the central Florida coast with a young fellow who insisted that he could save gas mileage by following very closely on the tail of semi-trucks. That he'd been drinking since early morning provided additional excitement. His muscle car had no seat belts—too much additional weight.

Two hometown expatriates had recently moved to Fort Lauderdale, and I took up sharing their apartment with its single piece of furniture (an outdoor chaise lounge), and a small TV raised off the floor on cinder blocks. The household's primary source of income derived from turning in beer bottles we'd emptied for their deposit value. I was trying to make Key West partially because I sought the whereabouts of a then obscure folksinger—Jimmy Buffett—and would offer him my services on mandolin and bass. It seemed to me that Jimmy had a pretty good deal. He didn't appear to wear shoes with any frequency, and if one can make a living barefoot, it seemed like an option to pursue.

I spent a few weeks in Fort Lauderdale, reading in the public library and walking three miles to the beach most days, taking in the five draft beers for a dollar lunch-time specials with my fellow dropout and one-night Bayou employee David, who was fleeing winter in Buffalo and also now sharing our minimalist digs. Then I hit the road for the Keys by thumb. That day the Dade County police stopped me three times trying to hitchhike through their jurisdiction, each officer imposing a sterner warning and implying more dire consequences for my scofflaw behavior. I think I tried to explain my plan to meet up with Jimmy Buffet to one of the constables, but he didn't know Jimmy. I got off the highway and retired to a local tavern on a side street, dug out some of my recycled beer can change, and drank up the nerve to play a few old songs on a borrowed guitar. As I was not offered a Tuesday night residency on the basis of my audition, I turned my whipped butt north all the way to CT.

Projector Rock

Broke, I found a minimum wage job in my hometown, working on the ground crew of a golf course. It was February and the ground was frozen, so I was put to work tuning two-cycle Harley Davidson golf cart engines, despite the fact that I didn't know a carburetor from a carbuncle. I covered for foreman Frank's three-hour liquid lunches and listened to AM radio. It was 1975. Pop music sucked—this was one thing Frank, who had kids my age, and Terry, my other garage mate and a raccoon-hunting native of central Pennsylvania—could agree on. So we listened to a local country station. Whatever happened to Moe Bandy? Joe Stampley? Mainstream Top 40 country music proved an antidote to the pop music of the mid-1970s.

Infected as I now was by exposure to bona fide country music in D.C. and Mel Tillis in daily doses, on Friday nights Stir Dudko and I frequented a bar on lower Main Street in Bridgeport, in a commercial dead zone around the corner from the bus station. The Brass Guitar was home to the only authentic country music in a fifty mile radius. A fairly ordinary Bridgeport bar—it was dark, of course, with figures at the bar bent at a permanent 45 degree angle over endlessly re-filled Schafer drafts. But if you kept walking past the bar and pressed through a swinging door, you entered a brightly lit space about the size of a large living room. A couple of wizened old cats with cowboy hats and string ties served as the house band—their set-up a rudimentary drum kit, a Japanese electric guitar, and a Sears Silvertone amp.

For no money down, the band offered the most disorganized and haphazard performance imaginable, which as a disorganized and haphazard young person naturally appealed to me. Stir and I were usually the youngest people in the room with several decades to spare. The homemade venue sported an open-mike, and over the course of an evening, a half-dozen middle-aged country music fans would stagger toward the house combo, straddle the microphone stand, and let rip. The resulting noise varied considerably, but these New England country & western fanatics had been waiting all week for this. We were especially attuned to the charms of Margie, a formidably rectangular woman of inscrutable age. Margie's performance would inevitably culminate in a *tour de force* version of "Bang My Box," during which she banged the walls of the narrow backroom where country music thrived in the heart of our fraying and dilapidated city.

Business proceeded as usual in the front bar, where everyone tried to ignore the fact that country music—or some mutant version—was playing within earshot. The front bar was populated by individuals who frequented Bridgeport's lower Main Street on a Friday night in 1975—citizens who had no real faith they would see 1976. A stranger once offered me a free sample from a Mason jar full of amphetamine. There were easily several thousand pills to draw on. But I was as awake as I could stand and passed on the offer.

A winter of stasis and alcohol-clotted slumber passed. One week at work we used a pressure hose to paint everything in the garage which needed to be green, and that week blowing my nose resembled a St Patrick's Day celebration. The next week yellow, the following, red. The ground began to thaw. I got to work daily at seven, liquor-induced headache like a lunchbox in hand. I dug ditches and turned the soil. I sang loudly while I mowed fairways. I could barely hear myself over the engine, so I assumed no one else could hear me. I sang Motown, late 60's soul, Johnny Taylor.

Now who's making love/to your old lady/While you been out/Making love?

I had sold almost all my musical instruments while going broke in D.C. I sold at discount the antique Gibson mandolin and was down to my $15 North Carolina pawn shop Kay electric, which wouldn't tune up and couldn't plug in. Though I was desperate to get some wheels, I dumped my first month's paycheck on a mid-60s Epiphone Casino electric, a Gibson-manufactured hollow-body guitar used for a short time by both John Lennon and George Harrison. A few months more hard labor and I was able to purchase a 1964 Volkswagon for $400. The heating system left something to be desired—I drove the five hours to D.C. one cold winter night in a mummy sleeping bag, downshifting at toll booths on I-95 with some difficulty. The accelerator had an embarrassing tendency to fully collapse to the floorboards at busy intersections, but I was now mobile and rigged for trouble.

A couple of us began to meet on Friday nights at an uninsulated summer cottage on Fairfield Beach. Stir had rented the place at bargain winter rates with several other Jesuit-trained ne'er-dowells. We banged our box to garage and R n' B classics. I didn't own an amplifier but was convinced by Cliff, a high school shade tree mechanic with whom I worked, that I could readily get a sound out of plugging into a movie projector he owned. He was right. It wasn't loud, but it was unusually nasty, a loud melodic flatulence, at least until the projector bulb burned out. After my stabs at bluegrass via Chuck Berry and acoustic guitar strumming, I was beginning to actually learn to play electric guitar. There were no longer any competent fellow musicians around to be intimidated by—my truly talented friends had passed me by and were elsewhere, getting paid to play music while I dug ditches and blew green snot out my nose. Nobody much was listening all that closely, except to hear what weird sound we could wrench out of the projector and the drum kit permanently erected in the living room of the beach shack. We considering trying to roll some film simultaneously, but unlike Joe Doy, we had no hot spools of *The Beatles at Shea Stadium* or anything else to play to.

Stellar was back on drums. He was learning to become a cook on the job and working hard to either stay on or off drugs, depending on the month and phases of the moon. Even if we'd had a microphone we didn't have anything to plug it into. The projector had only one input—manufacturers had not conceived of it multitasking as a PA system. So we yelled out lyrics at the top of our lungs. Nobody lived at the beach in the winter in those days so nobody complained. We were a goulash of influences striving to bloom into something viral.

Downtown

Six months after I'd repatriated myself to the Nutmeg State, I picked up a Village Voice in downtown Bridgeport which reviewed a New York band in such a way that they seemed to be embodying our play-it-through-the-projector aesthetic. Their promo picture promised a weedy bunch. Television was playing at Max's Kansas City, which Stir and I had made a pilgrimage to in 1973 to take in Doug Sahm and Bob Neuwirth.

While Manhattan presented a challenge to most of my comrades, I succeeded in enlisting two characters as marginal as myself to sally forth: Stellar and Cave N. Cave N. had shown an early interest in Black Sabbath in the midst of marathon consumption of LSD during high school. "Iron Man" really stuck to his ribs. But Cave N. on LSD was not all that much different from Cave N. unaltered by substances. He'd dropped out of Bennington in his sophomore year to drive a garbage truck for the City of Bennington—he may have received academic credit as well as a salary for this experiential education. In any case, the fall of 1975 found him back in CT, settled in once more with his mom, younger sister, and stock-broken father. Cave N. had in this period taken to wearing a uniform of sorts, a Bedouin headscarf and state police mirror shades. He was in fact the most gentle and even-tempered soul imaginable, but he looked like a member of the Manson family at large. Given Stellar's professional wrestler physique, they were good company to keep while roaming Gotham City.

Cave N. kept standing up from our table in the upstairs room at Max's in the middle of Television's set, pointing at Billy Ficca and insisting loudly to anyone within earshot that he drummed "just like Keith Moon." His enthusiastic commentary was unwelcome among the studied and pacific hipsters surrounding us. But we embraced our status as rubes in from the hinterlands and the Arabian peninsula for a big night on the town, full of lousy draft beer and free livestock-quality corn on the cob procured gratis at the Kettle of Fish.

A few months later, I deduced there was a bar on the Bowery in lower Manhattan that featured other Television-like bands. One weekend I gathered my weekly earnings and pointed my rickety VW toward the city to see what it was all about for myself. I paid three dollars at the door and wandered into the narrow confines of CBGB where the opening band was playing a limpid version of the Velvet Underground's "Pale Blue Eyes." The appeal of the band was the singer's Factory Girl looks and her vacant affect between songs. Blondie was playing mostly covers that night. What struck me was that I could actually imagine playing with similar competence. The Heartbreakers were the main attraction, though they were second billed. I'd been living in D.C. during the short heyday of the New York Dolls, but I'd worn through their first record and hyped their brand to anyone who would listen to me, which turned out to be no one in my acquaintance. There was good reason why I was in Manhattan by myself that evening. The Dolls' Johnny Thunders was the Heartbreakers calling card. Richard Hell—having recently been kicked unceremoniously out of Television—was their bass player. I was knocked backwards by the Heartbreakers' squall. After the set, Thunders narco-swaggered through the crowd toward the door in the narrow space next to CB-GB's long bar. We parted before Johnny like the Red Sea. I stepped in some dog shit left by Hilly Kristal's shaggy canine on the warped wood floor and retired to the medieval men's room to tend to hygiene.

The crowd cleared out after the Heartbreakers set. All the fine looking New York women I couldn't imagine approaching had followed Thunders and Hell out the front door and onto the Bowery like a fluorescent wake, which left me quietly sitting at a table in front of the stage with fifteen other geeks remaining in the club as the final band came on stage. The mild-looking lead singer held an acoustic guitar so cheap it had no brand name. The girl playing the outsized Fender bass against her slender frame stared across the stage at the side of the singer's head for the entire set. The drummer seemed to be the only conventional musician on stage, and the three of them together made a nervous racket very different from the disheveled rawk-in-role of the Heartbreakers. Their music was trebly and composed, the minimalist bass lines locking with James Brown-damaged guitar. A very white version of James Brown. Then again, the guitarist didn't seem to be attempting to channel the Godfather, but a young Tony Perkins.

It seemed he might have swallowed some of JB's fingernail clippings, however. His vocals came out high and choked, with a gun-against-the-neck intensity, on an odd match with a lyric palette which seemed to lean into a mundane, Andy Warhola style. This posture and what he was saying only came together in their last song, which grafted lyrics about a psycho killer to nonsense syllables absconded from an Otis Redding song. I wasn't quite sure what I'd just witnessed, but I liked it. I walked up to the lead singer a few minutes after the set and asked if he'd like a beer. He politely declined.

I dragged a few of my CT buddies down to CBGB's the next time the Talking Heads played. They were not impressed. And just when I thought I'd found the spawn of Maceo Parker and the Incredible String Band's Licorice in David Byrne. I left CBGB's that night with the sense that my tastes were drifting even further off tangent, if that was possible, up my own private box canyon.

This was manifested to me not long afterwards at the winter quarters of the Dirty Angels. George—who'd left his art major at Ohio University to become a full time guitarist—Joe Doy, and band mates Charlie and David had scored off-season rental of a fairly commodious beach house in Milford. It had all mod cons except central heating, which was the chief reason it was so affordable as a September-May sublet. Given that the boys were off playing and carousing until all hours, it worked out just fine. Spring was coming on and the snow had melted off the sand. The house's proximity to Milford harbor offered Joe Doy ample opportunity to exercise his kleptomania, the object of which at the moment seemed to be low horsepower outboard motors. He had a lot of them. Joe Doy would make George row him out to sea in the wee hours after returning from one ale house gig or another. A few rudimentary tools and some industrial wire cutters were all Joe Doy needed to get down to business on a given night. I sometimes wonder what became of all those 5hp Johnsons. But I don't wonder much. Joe Doy was all about process. He didn't much care for the consequences of mayhem, but in that regard, he was just a little bit out in front of the rest of us.

The Dirty Angels may not have the highest profile in rock history, but they were doing just fine at the time. They were the best we had, our representatives to an indifferent world, and we were proud of their accomplishments. Richard Gottehrer, who'd produced "My Boyfriend's Back," and written "Sorrow," who was in the Strangeloves, and who would go on to produce Blondie and the Go-Go's, was producing their inaugural disc and releasing it on his own label, Private Stock. This was big shit—our friends were just about rockstahs. Not that this procured them a house with central heating, but no deal is perfect. So us hangers-on, the wee folk, former neighborhood chums and Little League buddies come to be drop-outs and Sikorski employees, hamburger flippers and discharged vets, DWI hazards all, would gather for occasional evenings of drinking and ride-on rodeo, a sport which challenged an individual to hang on to the roof of an automobile careening wildly over beach sands after midnight. One evening, after a particularly pathetic performance at seven or eight rounds of Colonel Puck—a drinking game resulting in a rapid series of shots from a bottle of Southern Comfort—Joe Doy stumbled briefly from the room to return with a record that he assured was right up my twisted alley.

Joe Doy Frisbeed the first Ramones album across the shot-glass laden table to me. Gotttehrer had procured several advance copies of the Sire release for the band—it wouldn't see the light of day as a commercial release for another month. "You'll love this, Santa," Joe

Doy insisted. "It totally sucks." The front cover was intriguing. Four dorky leather boys in jeans and cheap boat shoes. The tallest, slouchiest one I'd seen lurking around the pool table at CBGB's. Having no inkling he was in a band, I can remember thinking: that is one weird-looking dude.

I hitch-hiked home from the Dirty Angel house the next morning—having destroyed my VW bug in a tequila fit several months earlier—in fuzzy-headed, cotton-mouthed anticipation. My sound system at the time was my little sister's Mickey Mouse close-and-play. Its needle resembled a dart board dart and hence proved a perfect match for the Ramones. I couldn't believe my ears, so I woke up Stellar and made him drive us down to the Fairfield beach shack. We threw down the Ramones album on a real stereo system and listened repeatedly in jaw-drop awe.

We heard the future of rock and roll, and it had absolutely no commercial potential. There was a spirited debate in regard to whether or not the whole thing was a joke. Well—if it was a joke, it was a good one. We could barely stop laughing, rolling on the floor, near to pissing ourselves. We kept turning the volume up louder and louder.

I made it down to CBGBs for the Ramones next date, a double bill with Television. My Jersey gal Dot was up for the trouble and high school bud Jared showed up with a rucksack directly from a wildlife field station in the Boundary Waters in Minnesota just as the Ramones first set began. The Ramones proved no joke. Not that we weren't laughing enough to spill half our beer in the twenty minutes they were on stage. But it was laughter about the preposterous genius and simplicity of it all. They'd boiled rock and roll down to a thick essence, serving it up at maximum speed with minimum theatre, which was—of course—its own theatre. Fifteen feet from the stage, their sound had physical force, obliterating and levitating during the brief duration of each song. It was like going to church, the alter boys all revved up, ready to go, in black leather and white tennis shoes.

I was making just enough in golf course maintenance to blow in a weekend, and I'd spent the late winter and early spring living at my uncle's uninsulated beach shack, showering outside when the need arose. But it was just not enough for me to stay afloat on. I was visibly spiraling the drain. Dot, who I met in a writing course I flunked, was a pinball wizard with almost as many problems as me, if that was possible. After waking up one Sunday morning in the bathroom of her dormitory wrapped in a shower curtain, I began to reflect on my life options as a 21 year-old with few skills and a propensity to drink to blackout. My stint with the one legitimate band I'd been allowed to join proved short. It was a blues band chaired by Dude's older brother Bob. Bob didn't fine us for playing wrong notes, but he would have liked to—and have made quite a sum in doing so. Bob attempted to run a tight ship, to demand a degree of discipline. It was a gallant but losing battle on his part. Playing our first date, the wines were too various, and after ripping off a rare and from all accounts stunningly impassioned solo on the Epiphone, I inadvertently stage-dived headfirst into the lap of a seated female patron, behavior which resulted in my firing as well as the firing of Stir Dudko for merely being associated with me.

I could just not see moving to New York. Too close to home. Returning to D.C. was too depressing an option. I'd struck out looking in the Capital. The abyss that had yawned open in the mid-70s in the absence of peace, love, and understanding looked plenty frightening from the lip, at least in the brief moments when I sobered up enough to peer into the excavation. I had a serious crush on Malcolm Lowry at the time—I was building my own volcano to crawl under. This was not going to end well. Add to that a notion that Hunter Thompson's *Fear and Loathing in Las Vegas* was a hornbook for modern manners and the wreck of my old 97 was on schedule. It was past my due date to get out of Dodge. Call me Ishmael and get me to the dock.

I looked into school options out west and managed to get accepted at San Francisco State despite my abysmal sophomore year in (or near) college. During the summer of 1976 I stopped pissing away my salary every Friday and Saturday long enough to save a semester's tuition, room, and board, with a hundred dollars to spare.

ACT III

Way Out West

Imagine a San Francisco where rents were cheap, a good portion of Haight Street boarded up with plywood and dark by 9pm, a town filled by day with side-burned business Johns and long-haired men and women in bell-bottoms and by night with nasty, speed-damaged drunks.

In 1976, dreams of a hip utopia were dead but not yet in the ground in San Francisco. Vestigial detritus from the Summer of Love lay about, some of it sentient, some inert. This I came to understand only after some time on site. The day I flew in I thought I'd landed in paradise. I was determined to move to San Francisco not to relive 1967 but because it was as far as I could get from the East Coast without a passport, and I neither had nor knew how to get a passport.

I arrived in San Francisco in late August with an Army surplus duffel bag of clothes and the Epiphone Casino. Into its hard shell case I managed to squeeze ten albums. The Ramones album made the cut, as did the Velvet Underground's 3rd, Gary Stewart's *Out of Hand*, Big Star, John Cale's *Paris 1919*, Richard and Linda Thompson's *I Want to See the Bright Lights*, and the Gram Parsons record I'd copped in D.C., him sitting, dead flowers and bottle at hand, poised for his audience with Keith Richards. I took a cab to a high-rise dormitory in the southwest corner of the city not far from Ocean Beach. The only person I knew in California was my high school friend Jim, who lived in Long Beach. He would soon be editing *Biker Lifestyle* under the handle Degenerate Jim and was my only connection in the Golden State.

When I'd filled out my preference form for roommates, I'd indicated that I was extremely anti-social, hard to get along with, and that I preferred a single room for the benefit and well-being of all parties involved. Instead of receiving a single, I was matched with the football team's starting offensive tackle, who decorated our shared digs in silver and black, including a radio shaped as an exact facsimile of an Oakland Raiders' football helmet. *Que sera, sera*—Tom and I got along fine. The friendly fellows next door took me camping in the Sierra foothills over Labor Day and after 24 hours announced that there was a guy back at school who I really had to meet—a stone Brian Eno fan with a closet full of platform shoes. Oh boy. I felt like the 727 I'd flown into San Francisco on had engineered some sort of time warp. I was not three hours behind East Coast time but three years.

The Brian Eno fan turned into my first California-bred buddy. Bill had grown up in Lompoc, where his father ran the state prison's laundry. Lompoc in 1976 was not a world-class wine-growing district but a slice of Middle America, distant and disassociated from either San Francisco or Los Angeles. I spent Thanksgiving in Lompoc where we walked after dark for hours through neighborhoods of flat, utilitarian homes and ornamental shrubbery. Bill did in fact have a closet full of platform shoes and a past penchant for glam rock of both L.A. and English origins, but he was attuned to recent rumblings from

London and the New York rock I'd been listening to for the past year and a half. The only recorded evidence which we had in hand were Patti Smith's *Horses* and the Ramones LP. Sometime before the end of the fall semester Bill managed to procure a copy of the Sex Pistol's "Anarchy in the UK" single. We subjected it to multiple listenings. My allegiance to the eclectic varieties of New York punk rock I'd been imbibing buffered some of my initial enthusiasm for English variations, which in the Sex Pistols case seemed derivative of the Ramones, the Dolls, and the Stooges in equal parts, all three of whom I'd been defending in the face of derision and indifference for years. In other words, the Sex Pistols were making exactly the music I would have made if I'd had the talent, will, temerity, desperation, and been English.

School/Dazed

I'd gone back to school as an English major. My reasoning—if I was going to crash and burn a second time, it might as well be while I was doing something I liked. Even though I'd flunked my first writing class back in CT due to overwhelming fear and stifling writer's block, I endeavored to get back in the saddle with an introductory, all-genre entry level writing class in the fall semester. The creative writing department was in fact what had lured me to San Francisco State University. Kay Boyle, novelist, activist, expatriate contemporary of Hemingway and Beckett, was on the faculty. Are you kidding me? To me she was a direct link to greatness whom I could rub up against. Or at least pass in the hallway, as she didn't seem to teach any classes. It turned out there were a cluster of great teachers, writers, and mentors on the faculty at SFSU then. I eventually took classes with the superb short story writer Gina Berriault (who introduced me to her partner Leonard Gardner, author of *Fat City*), Leo Litwak, late career author of the brilliant World War II memoir *The Medic*, straight-talking poet Dan Langton, and Nanos Valaoritis, a surrealist with a world-spanning vita, who entertained my obsession with Alfred Jarry. I still feel the loss of my Haight Street-purchased Jarry T-shirt, with its adage: "Live Fast, Die Young, and Deny Objective Reality." I had the fortune of scoring novelist Jim Leigh as my advisor. A musician himself, Leigh steered me around potholes I could not yet see. It was in many ways the exact opposite of my experience at the high-end university I'd landed in at 18, a lucky, fortunate do-over for me.

Twenty-two as my first semester at SFSU began, I was virtually enslaved to my influences. At the top of my reading list the previous year: Malcolm Lowry, Henry Miller, Lautreamont, Samuel Beckett, Thomas Pynchon, and William Burroughs. I was leaking fluid from all of them, but the degree to which Burroughs was weighing on me was only too evident. I offer extended evidence.

Deserted

A desert somewhere in the American Southwest. Observer's head is fixed in place by punji sticks dipped in rattlesnake venom and applied at both temples. Safari helmet three sizes too big rests on the sticks, shading the eyes. Body is buried up to the armpits but bare shoulders are greased liberally with QT. Observer chews carefully—watch those temple veins—on an entire pack of Trident Sugarless gum. Tin foil is still on the gum. Chews slowly.

On the plain within his vision appears a tribe of Bedouin, white-robed and riding camels, seated backwards, two to a camel. The man between the beast's head and first hump feeds a string of cartridges into a Gatling gun placed on the rear hump and operated by the second man, riding between the humps. Legs flail at the animal's sides goading them on, legs in irons, chains passing with little slack beneath the beast's lower neck and stomach, respectively. Several men have been shot and hang beneath their animals, swinging loosely between galloping legs. Camels with a front man down, hanging chained beneath the animal's neck, are having a rough time of it, heads hugging the ground like ostriches on the lam. Lone gunners fire wildly into the air. Gunners can't keep hot barrels off humps and are burning off camel hair. One passing hump is on fire, the beast screaming like a mandrake uprooted, the lead man hacking at the first hump with a scimitar, going for the water sac.

Hard behind this motley force T.E. Lawrence's boys. Some ride zebras, saddled and shoed for the occasion. A few have been fortunate enough to mount giraffes, perched right on the beast's head, hanging on to its shorn antlers like saddle horns fifty feet above the dusty ground. Others ride ostriches, erratic bearers who can only be controlled by insertion of a finger deep into their ear canals, indicating direction. A surprising number of men ride a horse costume. These steeds aren't holding up well. It's the slack between the head man and the ass man that's the problem. Some regulars waddle along, spread-eagle in the slack saddle position, firing then being knocked forward by the horse's ass, who often receives a rifle butt in the skull for his services. Other regulars are resigned to their position, riding the "animal" lying down, as in a hammock, firing as much at the hovering vultures as anything.

T.E. himself is riding a Harley, extended forks and hydraulic cushion shocks. He's smiling, but frankly looks silly in that nomad get-up of his. It's dangerous garb on that hog. His boys wear skintight khaki hot pants with matching halter tops, Vegas-style blackjack dealer caps, black argyle socks, and inexpensive Italian loafers.

The young teaching assistant running our class that first fall semester was not that impressed. What's going on here, she asked. Hmm. I thought that was the point—to create something which made it difficult to figure out *what's going on*. My influences were like a visible panty line, a mash-up of John Waters, Sam Peckinpah, Buster Keaton, and the Bonzo Dog Band? What can I say? It was of a piece with my pornographic Star Trek episode and my screen treatment for a range war between sheep and cattleman set in Dolores Park and the Castro. We wear other's garments until we can grow some of our own.

Hollywood Holiday

I accompanied my girlfriend Kerry to her family's San Fernando Valley home as the semester ended. I was giddy simply occupying a place on the planet where it was 70 degrees in mid-December. Palm trees swayed in the breeze adjacent to every Miramar Motel we passed on the coastal highway. Kerry was 19 and built for comfort, not for speed, the daughter of a Jewish father who owned a hardware store in Westwood and a mother busy pampering her cats. Once I saw how the cats had free range rights at the dinner table, sampling a bit from everyone's plate ala Chez Army Man, I felt a little more at home. For $100 I painted the stucco exterior of their house, a good deal for the family and a good deal for me, as I now had $110 in folding money after payment.

Having finished my work and worn out my welcome and utility, I finagled a ride down to Long Beach, where I set up camp with fellow CT expatriate Jim and his sainted girlfriend Candy. I got out of the way each day by hanging out on the beach, with its vista of oil rigs and elderly Jack LaLanne body builders, the only southern California individuals willing to countenance beach weather in the mid-60s. When I'd gotten enough sand in my notebook and teeth, I sauntered down the Long Beach boulevards to a cornucopia of thrift stores and pawnshops and carefully leafed through bin after bin of used vinyl.

I still possess my copy of Zal Yanovsky's *Alive and Well in Argentina*, a discovery I could not resist investing 99 cents in. I was similarly compelled to spend scant cash resources on James Brown's *I Can't Stand Myself When You Touch Me*, with its transcendently weird cover depicting the Godfather in a slick gray suit, standing in the blue ether at an oblique angle to three comely ladies, all equally untethered from earth-bound gravity and a flat plane of reference.

Jim spent several hours each day distributing *Biker Lifestyle* throughout the Los Angeles basin, but by midafternoon we could be found tucking into a new case of Lucky lager and repeatedly dropping the needle on Sonny Boy Williamson's "Santa Claus."

The police walked in/ and jarred me on the shoulder

What you doing with your hand/ in that woman's dresser drawer?

I said I'm just looking for what she got me/ for my Santa Claus

We played "Santa Claus" both for its innate holiday cheer and its ability to infuriate Jim's downstairs neighbor, to whom he did not wish good cheer. Laying the stereo speakers flat on the floor and playing Sonny Boy at full volume elicited the desired effect after the sixth or seventh iteration.

Kerry eventually drove down to Long Beach in her well-traveled 1966 Ford Fairlane to retrieve me and relieve Candy of putting up with Jim and I. Driving back north to San Francisco on 101 through Paso Robles and King City, we traced the Salinas River in the thin but still warm late afternoon January sunlight. I daydreamed of Jack Kerouac setting up camp in the dry river bed in his railroad brakeman days.

With thirty bucks in my pocket and no impending windfall in the offing, I could barely believe my good fortune.

In February my polka band lost to Dana Carvey at the dorm Talent Show. It might have been Carvey's first public performance. What a kick in the ass—I only knew Carvey as a quiet guy who walked around the dining hall in a Michelin Man parka holding hands with his girlfriend, and we had a hot clarinetist. Our second place finish, however, did give us the inside track for opening at a campus function later in the semester, on the condition that we lose the polka repertoire. We rebranded ourselves as Dallas Alice and the South of Market Meatpackers, nodding to Doug Sahm and Lowell George. The gig involved opening for Cornell Hurd and featured our bassist Danny driving a Triumph 750 up the handicap accessibility ramp into the dining hall and gunning the throttle at the appropriate moment during our rendition of "Leader of the Pack." Like Kiss, we were a band in need of gimmicks. But it was my first gig playing with drummer and fellow CT expatriate Jim Wade, with whom I would share the bouncing plywood stage of many a rock and roll venue over the next ten years. Jim brought his work compatriot Steve Hilton, who arrived all dressed up in a Russian sailor's suit. I'd begun to locate my people.

The City That Good Music Forgot

When I could scrape together five dollars in my first year in S.F., I'd grab the M-car from State after a day at the books and make it down to the Financial Zone, scarf free mini-franks and Cheez-wiz nachos in the downtown bars for the price of a draft, then walk up through Chinatown to North Beach, hoping for a whiff of Kerouac. Gutter-born restaurant offal and duck entrails trickling down the hill from Chinatown nixed that possibility, but I'd shamble up to The Saloon on Grant and drink 60 cent beers until I ran out of money. Columbus Avenue was all flashing lights and strip joint barkers plying their hype around Broadway, low-key fun and cheap thrills when you had nothing to spend. You could loiter in City Lights and record stores up Grant, browse through thousands of misplaced missives from past decades at the Postcard Shop, or just do walkabout with the other tourists, natives, sailors, and gender ambiguous citizens. Gregory Corso might be yelling and gesticulating across the street, audible from a block away, Bob Kaufman might pass in silence, a silence he'd kept religiously for years, Jack Micheline would be hanging at the front door of Vesuvio's, and Lisa Kindred pulling your cheap drafts at The Saloon. People I'd read or read about back East proved to be live action figures. I was a bit in awe of them all.

A punk rock scene began to spawn a few blocks from Grant sometime in early 1977. Its petri dish was the Mabuhay Gardens, down the street from Carol Doda's topless emporium at Columbus and Broadway and across the street from the sadly diminished Hungry I. The Mabuhay had just recently transformed from a Filipino supper club and maintained some of that club's tiki torches and tall-backed rattan chairs. Its punk shows were MC'd by a caustic ex-TV producer, Dirk Dirksen. Like Hilly Crystal at CBGBs, Dirksen did not meet hipness standards on most grounds. He was a middle-aged guy with a grown-in Hitler moustache, over-sized wire-rimmed aviator glasses, and a tendency toward Don Rickles' abusive rhetoric. There was plenty worth abusing. S.F. punk in its infancy was third generation spawn, with notable exceptions, like the hilarious, frenetic Mutants. Many bands were more influenced by the histrionics of London and L.A. headbangers than anything coming out of New York—mostly because there wasn't much coming out of the rich and eclectic New York scene which you could purchase at Aquarius Records on Castro Street, and there was not yet a couch surfing circuit to accommodate bands on the road coast to coast in 1977.

New York Rocker ran a piece about San Francisco: "The City That Good Music Forgot." It was a pretty superficial, tourist's appraisal of the SF scene. The interesting stuff in San Francisco frequently crossed boundaries into performance art, post-2am multimedia happenings, and agit-prop theatre which also incorporated some rock and roll moves, or at the least played in the same venues. The Dead Kennedys were basically a protest band, Phil Ochs on steroids. Did they catch Groovies' Roy Loney in the local production of Sam Shepard's *Back Bog*

Beast Bait? Sniff the invisible presence of the Residents or the grind of industrial precursors Rhythm and Noise, MX-80 Sound, or Chrome? The scene was also driven in many cases by the increasing visibility and politicalization of the gay community, whose presence was much more substantial and ingrained than it may have been even in lower Manhattan.

I did not catch many of the earliest Mabuhay shows—I was dead broke most of the time, working hard not to screw up once more as a college student. On that front, I continued into summer school after my first two semesters, making up for lost time and classes I hadn't bothered finishing several years earlier. After a summer subletting in Noe Valley, sharing an old Victorian with wannabe flower children and a beer drunkard (at $37/month rent), my new California-bred girl Lucia and I grabbed a studio in a Victorian a block and half from Market and Castro on 16th Street. I was going to school full-time, collecting $60 a week unemployment from the State of Connecticut and rehearsing most weekends with our now off-campus campus band. Dom, high school friend and Fats Domino piano acolyte, joined the group, as did our drummer Jim's Berkeley workmate Steve—who was in possession of a beat-up $50 Farfisa organ. Steve in turn dragged his high school buddy Cory into our orbit. You've got to meet Cory, he kept telling me. I did one Friday evening. Cory shook my hand firmly and wouldn't let go. Within a minute we were in a furniture-smashing wrestling match in the living room of Steve and Jim's 9th Avenue apartment, bouncing off the plate glass living room window.

Steve and Cory had two abiding musical passions—Krautrock and obscure rockabilly. The Krautrock did not stick to my ribs like the Farmer

Boys or Billy Lee Riley, but it was a weird soundtrack nonetheless, which reached its natural marriage in a version of Hank C. Burnette's "Don't Mess With My Ducktail" sung phonetically by a Swedish rockabilly cat whom Cory had uncovered. Burnette's signature phrase really hit the spot: "Done mess mit mein ducktail!" OK, buddy—I wouldn't *dream* of touching your toup. In a pre-networked world, these discoveries took some real effort. I dropped in one night to find Cory on the phone with Warren Smith, the man responsible for foisting on innocent American youth blasts like "Ubangi Stomp" and the proto-emo love lament "A Red Cadillac and a Black Moustache" back in the mid-50s. Cory had somehow tracked Warren down to his gig as night watchman at an East Texas oil refinery and shot the shit with him for the better part of an hour.

My projector rock episode aside, I hadn't really played in a rock band with any regularity since early high school. In the basement on 9th Avenue, our lingua franca was mid-60s one-hit wonders, the odd Sun Studios song, the Stones, the Beatles and the Stooges' "Fun House." We were just proficient enough to eschew punk rock incompetence. We set up like the Band—organ, piano, bass, drums and one guitar, but I was no Robbie Robertson. If we'd had the uniforms, we would have gladly suited up as Paul Revere and the Raiders—we covered several of their hits. We called ourselves the Blemphrions, care of a sci-fi novel race of individuals who thrived without heads.

The only bar that would have us sat out on Taraval, a few blocks west of 19th Avenue. It was so far from the madding crowd that the owner agreed to let us play a month of Saturdays. But he would not agree to pay us until he determined our capacity to draw a crowd of boozers. We worked on that our first Saturday date and drew some friends, but no dough was forthcoming. The second week we tried to negotiate some cash upfront. No traction—let's see how you do, says the barkeep. Okie doke—here's how we do. We proceeded to drink our way through copious quantities of free bar drinks for four sets. The next week we invited everyone we could think of with a promise—the first drink's on us. We were ordering beverages by the half dozen, before and after each set. Scores of drinks. Hundreds, eventually. After the final set, Dom and I had a seat at the bar and ordered six shots of schnapps for the two of us. Later that night nine of us made it back to 9th Avenue in and on girlfriend Lucia's Corvair, drum kit filling the back seat. Our benefactor cancelled our final Saturday. Our cost was beyond his means.

Several months later I drifted to southern California with Lucia for a family affair in Thousand Oaks and realized in transit that my stay north of L.A. coincided with several Dirty Angels dates in L.A. Local boys made good, the Dirty Angels had just signed to A & M and were playing an outdoor date at UCLA with the Talking Heads, followed by two nights at the Whiskey a Go Go with Arthur Lee and his newest incarnation of Love. This was the big time. I couldn't make the UCLA gig, but contacted Degenerate Jim in Long Beach and arranged to rendezvous with George at the Tropicana.

The Tropicana was, of course, a notorious lodging option for rock-stahs by 1978. The Dodgers Sandy Koufax had bought the place and spruced it up in 1962, and that's about the last time major repairs were endeavored. Jim Morrison had graced the site in his leather pants in the late 60s. Tom Waits had lived there and conducted all business in the phone booth between the pool and the coffee shop. The Dirty Angels on arrival had been greeted with a gift from the A & M office—a case of Mogen David wine.

The Ramones were on site when I arrived around noon. The Dirty Angels had shared a number of dates with the Ramones in the Northeast over the previous few years. George spoke of how drummer Tommy Ramone would hang out in their dressing room because the other Ramones regularly beat him up. Brotherly love—you don't want to miss it. I'm not sure who was packing into the Mogen David, but by late afternoon we were well into our second fifth of vodka in George's second floor room. I found myself sitting at the end of George's bed next to Dee Dee, passing an open bottle of Smirnoff between us, watching cartoons on the black and white TV about three feet in front of us. At one point Dee Dee simply pitched forward off the bed, his head bumping the screen, keening him back to consciousness. Things got fuzzy.

I must have slept this off at some point, as I recall the backstage scene at the Whiskey, shaking hands with Arthur Lee. Even in my vodka-numbed semi-consciousness, I was both excited and acutely aware of how peripheral I was. The Dirty Angels acquitted themselves, a well-oiled rock machine, but it was a Love crowd here in Arthur Lee's hometown. Back at the Tropicana, Joey Ramone heroically endeavored the outdoor steps up to the second floor landing. Degenerate Jim mounted his Harley for a trip back to Long Beach, against all sage advice. He totaled the bike and his left leg not far down the road, and walked for the next three decades with a limp. It was all a bit much. Lucia rescued me the next morning in her oil-burning Corvair and we retreated north to the safety of San Francisco.

Burning Autos Bring You So Much More

I finished school in May and was having enough success that I decided to stay on the horse and enter the M.A. program in writing at SFSU. That fall I answered an ad on the wall at Aquarius Records—someone was looking for a guitarist to write melodies to words—and that sounded like something I could do. I called the number I plucked off the wall and auditioned over the phone to Michael Goldberg, who was serving in managerial capacity for someone else. This was a first for me—my experience was that musicians simply fell in with each other, like so many stray hyenas wandering the veldt in search of a pack.

The call resulted in a meeting on the second floor of a Victorian on Page Street in the Haight with the talent in question. Nadine was the daughter of an English father and a Honduran mother. She sported an Afro, a resume dotted with strip clubs, and wrote poetry she wanted to sing. My job would be to provide the melodies.

I thought Nadine's lyrics were good, lending themselves to setting a riff behind them and fashioning an odd chorus to accompany verse. My favorite was "Van Gogh's Ear."

Life/Can be so painful/And death/So severe.

No shit. I was too unschooled in American poetry, despite my recent B.A. in English, to realize Allen Ginsburg had riffed on Van Gogh's ear or absence of same in the not distant past. But real artists don't copy—they steal, right? Or so said William Burroughs, in *Creem* magazine to boot. Nadine and I met once a week over the course of the fall and eventually churned out a set of songs.

It was time to flesh these sketches out. I enlisted Jim Wade on traps then went looking for a bassist and another guitar player. I'd met a fellow in my Spanish class at State who claimed to be a bass player, Jim Gordon. We enlisted Jim's buddy Gary to play lead. The two of them were just out of their teens, Bay Area natives, more enamored of the Grateful Dead than the law should allow. But we gathered together in a rehearsal space over the Stud on Folsom and Nadine and I more or less beat them into submission. No solos longer than eight bars. Pick up the tempo. Keep the tempo. Stop smoking so much dope—failed there. Nadine had a drill instructor side to her, and the instruction went tolerably well. We worked up "Van Gogh's Ear" and our other hits, throwing down sixes of Olympia to lubricate the gears. The rehearsal studio had no plumbing, so after requisite lager from Sky Blue Waters, we'd muscle our way to the trough at the back of the Stud or head down the block to Febe's, where the men's room sported Folsom Street's best advertisements for used, assless leather chaps. I tried to talk us all into a band uniform grounded in the availability of these stylish togs. Nadine and I were out-voted two to three. We could of beaten S.F.'s Buck Naked (RIP) and the Bare-Bottomed Boys to the finish by five years, but our boys just couldn't make the leap.

I think Jim G. suggested we call ourselves the Exploding Pintos. Jim was a car guy—it never would have crossed my mind. Some Johnny-Rottens-come-lately later made off with our tag. But Exploding Pintos matched the zeitgeist of San Francisco, early 1979. The mayor had been shot. Harvey Milk had been shot. Everything flamed, up and out.

Coming up with band names is fun and easy. Getting gigs is not. Nadine's new roommate JE took on the thankless task of managing us. JE was British and had spent some time at the Royal Military Academy Sandhurst. Given his permanently amused and louche perspective on the human parade, it was not surprising JE did not receive a commission in service to her Majesty. But his accent and affect were sufficiently charming to open some doors in San Francisco. There was rarely money behind these doors, but that was about what we expected.

We played a few times at the Mabuhay. Dirk Dirksen insulted us in introduction. On what grounds I can't recall, but as he insulted everyone who darkened the stage of the Mabuhay, we felt at home. Ice cubes flew at us from the shadows as we ran through our set—this yet another signal of love and acceptance. JE got us on the very bottom of the Rock Against Racism bill at the Temple Beautiful, recently vacated by Jim Jones' clan. The Dead Kennedys headlined. Few saw our afternoon set, but we cast our vote.

Warehouse gigs followed. One was at a vast three story factory on 3rd Street, the former home of American Can. Bruce Conner seemed to inhabit the space we played in—I mounted the stairs with guitar and amp in hand to find him doubled over in voiceless laughter outside the front door of the space. We were on a double bill with the Fleshapoids, whose calling card was their 7" single, "Nuke the Whales." The band was decked out in Sid Vicious regalia, dyed black hair spiked, a thick metal chain and padlock around the lead singer's neck. How could Van Gogh's ear compete with this display of authenticity? We all had a few too many plastic cups of gratis draft swill, and again piled into lovemate Lucia's Corvair, our defacto gig bus. A wrong turn in search of 3rd Street landed us on a set of rail tracks, the dimensions of which fit the wheelbase of the Corvair to a T. Off downtown we motored for a mile, like an SP maintenance truck working the graveyard shift.

Our warehouse gigs dried up. We had some songs on tape, but no money to release them in any format. We weren't punk rockers, but we were a long way from the mainstream. Our performances did not raise fanfare beyond the base of our loyal friends. Nadine—who you might think would have some stage chops given her time pole dancing—was an indifferent lead singer. I got it—she was a poet. But somebody needed to make show. Jim Gordon—a ringer for a young Muammar Gaddafi—came the closest, but he'd swallowed a bit too much Don Kirschner stadium rock. Sometimes dorm buddy Mark Soden would sit in on bass. Mark's dry sensibility was a nice spin, but we couldn't quite get up the ladder.

The Exploding Pintos sputtered to a stop. Without Nadine, we picked up some weekend gigs at Gullivers, a bar at the point where Grant Street splits off from Columbus, in the heart of North Beach, across Grant from The Saloon. There was no cover and we weren't getting anything from the bar except all we could drink. But Jim

Wade worked the crowd for tips so relentlessly from his drum stool that the take from a constantly circulating hat in the audience was much more than we were accustomed to making at the Mabuhay. With no cover, on a main thoroughfare, on Friday nights the place was packed with both locals and tourists. Jim Wade and I knew scores of Beatles songs, and we played most of them, as well as garage rock like the Standells' "Dirty Water," Chuck Berry's "No Particular Place to Go," and multiple Stones covers. We didn't rehearse this stuff, so the added element of forgetfulness and human error added to the charge. When we finished up our fourth set at 1:50 we would hector barkeep JT as we packed up our gear until he gave us a bottle of Jack Daniels or a similar door prize. Then we'd stumble down the hill to Clown Alley, where a grill man who was a dead ringer for James Baldwin would serve up hamburgers with everything and all the pickles we could eat. For a summer, Gulliver's was our Kaiserkellar and North Beach our Reeperbahn. And I guess we were the Swinging Blue Jeans.

My prose writing was going through a dry spell. Lovely Lucia departed for greener pastures—I couldn't blame her. I was in grad school at SFSU full-time, working at an import warehouse at Folsom and 9th four days a week, and trying to front a band. I was working way too much to commit on any front. I'd look out on the freighters on the Bay from the top of the hill where I lived on 16th Street with a strong desire to be shanghaied.

Rooms to Move

Pintos on permanent hiatus, I took to perusing the bulletin board of Aquarius Records again. There I found a posting that piqued my curiosity: a guitarist/songwriter enamored of Mersey beat looking for same. This was stuff that ran pretty strong in my musical DNA, the stuff I was listening to when I was 12, wondering at the wonder of pop songs. I gave a call, and we agreed to meet out at SF State.

Buzz was mop-topped and indeed well-versed in the pop of our early youth. We shared an admiration not just for the usual suspects (read: Beatles), but stalwarts on the periphery—the Searchers, Gerry and the Pacemakers, Billy J. Kramer. This was not the fodder and feed of San Francisco's punk community, but it was where we both lived. We made a date to meet with guitars.

Despite the fact that I'd co-written a set of Exploding Pinto's tunes with Nadine in late 1978, I did not consider myself a songwriter. Melodies, sure, no problem. But the whole package? I was working to prove I had some talent as a storyteller in my grad school program, but in no way saw myself a poet, and for better or worse I equated lyrics with poetry. Nonetheless, I occasionally got into enough of a trance state strumming my Epiphone to stream a few lines, a chorus or a couplet. Back in CT to see the family at Xmas, I descended into Dude's basement in Bridgeport a few days after New Year's with

George and Stellar in tow to cut a song of mine to Dude's four-track reel-to-reel. The song, "Girls' Eyes," was a kind of story. There was a snippet of my old CT gal Dot in there—she, the pinball wizard—and I had begun to understand that rather than approach lyric writing as some sort of bastardized poetry, I could paste little narrative and descriptive bits together from a slant perspective, and get away with something not too embarrassing.

The model singer-songwriter we all came up with in the early 70s was James Taylor—deeply confessional and heart on his sleeve. There was zero distance between the man singing the song and the lyric's tale. If a handful of creative writing workshops had taught me anything, it was that that was an unnecessarily narrow approach to narration. My vocal was Richard Hell damaged, but I put my first guitar solo down on tape and as a piece the song had a pulse. I send a cassette to Bomp's Greg Shaw who forwarded the tape to *New Yorker Rocker*'s demo column and they actually reviewed it.

Stellar was not on drums that night, but he was down with us in Dude's basement, shouting along with me in the chorus of "Girl's Eyes." He looked healthy and was in good spirits, but I flashed back to a time three years previous when I watched him cook up and shoot dope before we could head out to New York City.

Writing this now, I recall a summer evening a few weeks before we started high school. We were at a church fair in Shelton, and Stellar and I were on the Ferris wheel. We'd had our merry-go-round above the crowd, and then the Ferris wheel operator jerked the wheel to a stop, allowing people to disembark. The bucket Stellar and I sat in stopped at 10:30 on the sun dial, just beyond the apex of the spinning wheel, looking out over the fairground and families, the Potatuck graveyard of Riverside Park, and the Housatonic River. Valley dwellers milled and ate pink and blue cotton candy, eighth grade couples nuzzled each other in the shadows of old trees crippled by a century of industrial effluent, volunteer firemen raked in pitched coins, an on-duty and an off-duty cop walked side by side through the midway past the spinning cups and bumper cars and the sledgehammer test of strength drawing greased up and acned youth.

Stellar abruptly stood up from our Ferris wheel seat, spread his arms like Christ, and screamed at the top of his lungs: *GOD HELP ME!* Heads swiveled, gazes shot up. Cops and firemen froze. Stellar had dropped back in his seat, looking around, as if the blood-curdling shriek had emerged from somewhere else. And it had. But unless you'd been starring directly at him when he let loose, you'd never have known. The Ferris wheel operator knew more by deduction than anything, as we were obscured from below by several buckets imposing themselves between the operator and the source of anguish and depravity. The Ferris wheeler gave Stellar a deadpan stare but otherwise kept his counsel as he raised the bar and allowed us to disembark. Why was it Stellar who got the second degree? Wasn't I even on the short list? Who was I? Don Knotts?

Yes I was. Two cops stood at the base of the Ferris wheel, eying us skeptically, the odd couple—the hulking, muscled youth and the pencil-necked geek.

GOD HELP ME! Coming from Stellar, this was both a command and a query.

Nine months after our basement recording, in the fall of 1979,

George found Stellar in the front seat of his car outside a club in New Haven with a needle still in his arm. Jim never woke up.

By the time Buzz and I met to play together, I'd begun to work up a few other songs. Buzz already had a bunch, and they were very good songs. I slipped easily into vocal harmony with Buzz and faked my way through eight-bar guitar breaks. It felt like there was something of substance there. There wasn't anyone in town doing anything like what we seemed ready to jump into, other than the Flamin' Groovies, who didn't count as they were already stars in our heads and a bit older anyway. Now we needed compatriots for our combo.

I brought along Steve, with his beat-up Farfisa organ. Steve was already playing at the Mabuhay as organist with new wavey Novak, but that was not exactly keeping him busy. Buzz brought in a buddy of his, Tim. Tim had migrated south from Redding to attend SF State and with hometown friend Scott Ryser formed the Units, who gained some notoriety with their synth-grounded attack. But Tim had recently purchased a huge marching drum, bought a foot pedal, a snare, and a wood block, and was a month into teaching himself to hit them in time and tandem.

We met to feel each other out at China Blue, a rehearsal studio on Second Street down near China Basin, run by a graying fellow everyone referred to as Doc. The city's methadone clinic and Cutter's Bar were a block away. Cutter's was a throwback to the time San Francisco had a working waterfront, and free baloney sandwiches were always on tap. We set up in one of China Blue's spartan chambers—two electric guitars in the hands of two rhythm guitarists, a Question Mark and the Mysterians drone from Steve's Farfisa, and Tim on his couple of drums. We ran through a bunch of Buzz's songs, some rockabilly covers, and a song or two of mine, and decided after our two hours were up that we didn't need a bass. Steve was covering that with his left hand, and a bass would just get in the way. Of what, we weren't sure, but we liked the trebly sound. Cymbals—of which Tim had none—and heavily amplified bass impulses take up a lot of bandwidth. We favored open spaces between sounds.

Part of what was attractive about punk was the physicality of its frontal assault—the sound itself would just blow you back, and part of the fun was fighting that headwind, the thrill of walking in the wind tunnel again the blast. We'd all had a mouthful and enjoyed it, but had no interest in replicating the experience. While we wanted to exercise and evoke the same energy, we wanted to do so in service to a song, at half the volume. Re-imagine the Ramones as a skiffle band, Dee Dee on tea chest bass, Tommy with just two drums and a wood block. We wanted to insinuate ourselves, underwhelm you.

After a few months figuring out how to play together, we demoed a couple of Buzz's songs in his friend Arnie's garage in North Beach before we began looking for gigs. Steve was traveling that month with a jar of White Crosses, hoping to take off a few pounds. We cut the speed with Lucky Lager in quantity, and the results were predictably skittery. Rather than view the recording as an aberration, we took it as a template for how we ought to sound, all the time.

Needing a name to hang on this business, we settled on a message flashed from a small neon sign in South Park, then a hobo haven with a perpetually burning 55 gallon drum in the middle of its small oval public space. We passed through South Park on the way to the grocery on 3rd Street where we bought beer before China Blue sessions from the milky-eyed counter clerk. 84 ROOMS the sign claimed. Really? That kind of capacity in a two story wood-frame residence? Mighty tight quarters, down where Kerouac used to set up before missing his milk run on the Burlingame freight. It was years before we figured out that 84 was the South Park address rather than the name of this SRO venue.

In late 1979 we finally talked our way into a gig. It was at the Roosevelt on Market Street, a block up from South Van Ness. This was not exactly the center of San Francisco's entertainment district—the neighborhood's calling card was a Zim's down the street, and the Roosevelt made its money off lunch trade. One of the lunch waitresses—Robin—had convinced the owners to host bands on Friday and Saturday nights, a convenient way for Robin to get her own fledgling band the Sponges a gig. Robin's partner Scott was a Sponge.

Scott had been drummer for the Who for an evening. Keith Moon had taken the stage a few years earlier at the Cow Palace, S.F.'s big rock and rodeo venue, and proved after several songs of inebriated flailing incapable of serving as the Who's percussionist that night. Keith was escorted off stage and Pete Townsend, in the-show-must-go-on mode, asked for volunteers from the audience. Scott stepped up, plopped down on Keith's stool, and kept his time.

Our initial gig was set for December 28, 1979, the last weekend of the decade. The Sponges would open, 84 Rooms would follow, and local punk celebrity Mary Monday, auteur behind "I Gave My Punk Jacket to Rickie," would headline.

The size of the crowd that Friday night surprised us. Mary Monday had her fans and the Sponges their friends, but an awful lot of people that Buzz or Steve or Tim or I knew were apparently curious about how we'd manage. My future spouse of 26 years was in the crowd, but I hadn't met her yet. I can recall standing in the Roosevelt's kitchen, behind the stage, chorgling beer in preparation for our debut. We gulped and went on—people pointed to Tim's drum kit, laughing. Where's your bassist? We had borrowed a friend's Fender Twin Reverb, and Buzz was playing Michael Goldberg's Gretsch, still on loan from the inception of the Exploding Pintos, but what little we owned of what was on stage was vintage Sears gear, not because that was hip, but because we couldn't afford any better. We ramped into Buzz's' "You Send Me" at amped up, White Cross speed and the crowd moved—up, down, sideways. Steve and I sang "Slow Down," not the Larry Williams' burner of Beatles' trade but the Sun Records cut by the rockabilly baker, Jack Earls. Tim sang his tribute to JB and wife KB, "High Blonde Pressure," and I my paean to cuckoldry, "(You're My) Babysitter." We sweated copiously and we didn't suck.

Later that night I went downstairs to divide the door with the Sponges and Mary Monday. Even at two bucks a head, there was a good pile of money by the standards of a scene where you usually ended up playing for free after settling the bar tab. Robin, the de facto manager of evenings at the Roosevelt, suggested a 20/30/50 split, Mary Monday taking half of the night's proceeds.

"No—demanded Monday—I'm taking it all."

Huh?

"I *need* it all." She proceeded to sweep off the singles and fives spread out in three neat piles on the table and stuff the take into the pockets of her leather jacket, which Richie had apparently returned to her. Robin, Scott, and I stood there with our mouths hanging open as Mary Monday stomped up the stairs. I guess it turned out we were more hippies than punks. My band members took the news surprisingly well, laughing it off. We were drunk on free draft beer and were a band on the rise.

Our second gig was at a bar on Polk Street without a stage. I was so drunk I flipped over a three foot railing in the midst of our set. Maybe we peaked early.

Summer of Love Redux

For a brief moment we were the flavor of the month. As noted earlier, there weren't a lot of groups playing Mersey beat rock at amphetamine pace in San Francisco in 1980. All four of us sang and wrote, though Buzz wrote more than the other three of us combined. But we were a democratic collective and we split the spotlight—40 watt though it may have been. We were in fact all over the place in terms of influences. My soft spot was the garage rock and one-hit wonders of my early youth, e.g. the Swinging Medallions' "Double Shot of My Baby's Love." In my mind, I thought I probably had one hit song in me, tops. Steve wrote space age instrumentals to supplement his on-going rockabilly fixation. Tim's admiration for reggae of a political bend was manifested in his cover of Burning Spear during many of our live dates. To further confuse matters, we'd often cover Hank Williams and the Fugs' "C.I.A Man" in the same set.

We spent a few afternoons in the summer of 1980 putting down tunes to Tom Mallon's eight track reel-to-reel in his Cole Valley living room. Set up a guitar amp in the bathroom, drums in the kitchen. Each of us chose a song. The results were quite listenable but—as suggested above—eclectic as a piece. What kind of band are you? We took to replying, "skiffle, ska, and scum."

We were most *simpatico* playing with Flamin' Groovies off-shoots like Roy Loney and his Phantom Movers or the Kingsnakes, or the mostly-brother, mostly-bespectacled band No Sisters, but we appeared with just about anyone. We opened for Chris Isaak at Rock City shortly after he'd moved to town. Actually it was Silvertone we opened for, a trio featuring Isaak on guitar and vocals but named for its drummer John Silver, who had recently departed the Dils with some degree of name recognition. JE got us a gig at a staff party for the *Whole Earth Catalog*, where we suffered our first and last experience of Styrofoam sword fencing with Mountain Girl. We did a completely unplugged gig at the Mabuhay, standing in a line at the front of the stage with two unamplified acoustic guitars, a snare drum, and accordion. In 1980, this precipitated a mixture of catcalls, chucked ice-cubes, confusion, and wonder, and even seemed to throw Dirk Dirksen off his game a bit. We opened at Berkeley Square that fall for the ballyhooed but then unrecorded Go-Go's. The local fanzine *Forget It!* described the proceedings.

> *Friday's show started with a band called St. Regis, who have a lot of expensive keyboards and synthesizers. They can play OK but they have a shitty stage show. Booooring. Next up was 84 Rooms from San Francisco. They have a strange set-up to say the least: the drums consist of bass, snare, hi-hat, one cymbal, and a wood block; there's an ancient Farfisa organ and two guitars. 84 Rooms is great! They are like the Rezillos in a way, a sort of teen-beat, beat pop dance music. There is also a touch of rockabilly. This is a band to see if you like dancing even a little bit.*

We'd hoped to schmooze with the Go-gals backstage, but the Go-Gos sequestered themselves behind closed doors—the only member of the band who would give us the time of day was bassist Margot Olavarri, who was soon to leave the group. After the gig, in the wee hours of the morning, I found myself at a party at Kevin Hunter's SF loft, down near South Park. Hunter—like the Go-Gos—would soon enough be on the rise with his band Wire Train. Buzz and I stood stupidly against a wall of the loft sipping on our Tree Frog beer, staring at the Go-Gos leaning against their own wall across the room. I felt like I was back at a junior high dance, paralyzed, incapable of moving. So much for the personal magnetism and high-powered sex life of an aspirant garage rock star. I was actually the only member of the band at this moment not living with a romantic partner, and in time I managed to get myself in sufficient trouble as a result. Did you ever have to make up your mind John Sebastian had asked in my teen days. Sebastian couldn't, and neither could I. Go-Gos aside, my market value as a boyfriend had increased significantly after our first Roosevelt gig.

In the spring of 1980 we were making almost enough money playing to forego other employment, but that interlude was brief. That summer I joined Steve working as a shipping clerk for the Xandria Collection, a sexual aids retailer. Before long, Buzz also secured work at Xandria. There were only five of us working in shipping, so members of 84 Rooms represented a quorum. An equal number of employees worked in the front office, minus honchos Roy and Gaye Raymond, who had a separate office suite. Roy and Gaye were well-put-together Bay Area professionals, Stanford grads, in their 30s.

They spoke to Xandria's customers in our catalog as Ray and Judi Lawrence. Their bedside manners were pleasing, friendly, welcoming. They also owned newly born Victoria's Secret, but their cash cow at that time was Xandria.

The novelty of filling postal boxes with thrusting penises and vibrating butt plugs mostly wore off after a few days. But compared to my previous shipping position, packing Balinese hand puppets and other exotica, the shift to erotica had a peculiar appeal. Most of our merchandise was produced in Hong Kong but arrived at our Xandria outlet at the foot of Portrero Hill from Doc Johnson in L.A. Doc trafficked in all things dildoesque. The product came packed in shredded copies of pornographic novels, which we would reassemble piecemeal with each new shipment, like one of Dickens' serial novels.

Pulling an 18" double-headed dong from its warehouse bin, shaking it in your fellow shipping clerk's face, bending it like Beckham, we knew our products were winging to soon-to-be satisfied customers. Usually somewhere in Utah, if the informal geographic distribution chart we maintained in the back room was accurate. The position afforded the option of mailing selected items to former lovers in plain brown envelopes, *sans* return address or other indicators of source. Xandria's inventory also provided unique prizes for a dance contest we held one night at a gig in the Haight. But the correspondence which sometimes accompanied orders could feel like we were living an X-rated version of *Miss Lonelyhearts*.

The day I came out our back door to throw some boxes into our dumpster and found a ten year-old dumpster diver racing off down 16th Street trailing Joni's Butterfly by its wires, I knew I'd almost had my fill. After six months in the sex trade, I left to take a position at a cavernous Southern Pacific warehouse down on 3rd Street. I worked for non-union wages but the hours were flexible and it was tolerable work as work goes.

I felt like we were going somewhere as a band, but maybe we were going in four directions at once. As the Beatle said: all things pass. Tim was the first to peel off. His musical tastes were less reflected in our headlong trajectory toward perfecting the perfect two-minute, electric-guitar-driven pop nugget. He was a little calmer than the rest of us as well, happy at home, less happy drinking all night in a smoke-filled bar, waiting to get paid $15 three hours after you played. I became so irritated one night over sitting for an hour past closing time for our portion of the door that I started dropping potted plants to the floor of the genteel joint we were in. I was no Mary Monday, but I acted out when provoked. Churlish behavior aside, we were a delicate mechanism, and without Tim we trotted forward like a three-legged dog.

Finding a drummer to fill Tim's slot proved a challenge. The anxiety deriving from this put Steve and Buzz at loggerheads, which came to bursting point a few months later at another Berkeley Square gig, which proved Buzz's last. Oddly enough (or not), we continued to function as friends socially outside the band pretty well, collaborating in our Rackit Records collective for some years to come. But 84 Rooms in its original and purest iteration disintegrated at that moment. Three-legged dogs can make their way. Two-legged dogs struggle without prosthetic assistance.

Please Release Me

After a few months of thumb twirling, Steve and I became a bit stir crazy. Steve was now driving for Yellow Cab, continuing to record strange cover versions of popular hits of our youth by bouncing takes between two old Wollensach reel-to-reel tape machines. I'd finished my coursework and exams at SFSU but was not making any progress finishing a thesis. Steve and I began slowly assembling 84 Rooms 2.0. We enlisted Exploding Pintos Jim W. and Jim G. as our rhythm section with Pinto Gary on lead guitar and began rehearsing irregularly at China Blue. It was a weird transitional period—we'd lost Tim but some of his Jamaican influences had rubbed off on us. And in San Francisco in 1981, the dance music you heard at the Stud was pervasive. I wrote a handful of songs that attempted to capitalize on the musical chops of the two Jims and Gary. We played this stuff with a degree of energy and competence, but they were forgettable, throw-away tunes. I missed Buzz's capacity to turn out quality songs at will, which had meant that Steve and I only had to throw in a tune of our own now and then.

But as with many who had proceeded us, and especially in this newly burgeoning era of DIY recording projects, we didn't let a paucity of fine new tunes bridle our ambition to get a record out. We were clearly frustrated by the fact that we'd actually had an album's worth of strong material when Tim and Buzz departed.

We went into Hyde Street studios late in 1981 with three songs—a guitar instrumental of mine which seemed to have some potential as a dance tune, a song of Steve's in which he got to trot out the trombone chops he had worked up in the Michigan State marching band, and a rockabilly deep cut released by Roy Orbison's diminutive side-kick Peanuts Wilson, recorded by Norman Petty in Clovis back in 1957. We recorded as a duo plus Jim Wade. We would gladly have had Jim officially on board, but as the best musician among us he was in demand, and at the time on a retainer with a rock band fronted by Fleetwood Mac-singer-for-a minute Dave Walker, an arrangement allegedly backed by Marin County coke money. Why were we in Hyde Street—an actual professional recording studio frequented by actual rockstahs? We might have been working at some sort of reduced hourly rate, and we worked awfully quickly, but it was expensive. Nonetheless, I imagine our studio fees in full were equivalent to what Mick Fleetwood was paying at the time to get a proper kick drum sound. The members of Fleetwood Mac, however, were not driving a forklift and a jitney to finance their work. Recording stretched in bits and pieces into 1982, but Steve and I were reasonably satisfied with the results. We added two of our songs from the 1980 Tom Mallon living room sessions and felt we had something like a viable 12" EP in hand.

Meanwhile, we were beginning to play out a bit as a five piece band. We did a gig at a spring bacchanal for the art department at the UC Santa Cruz campus. To fill three sets, we dug deep into Blemphrions cover material and songs from gigs at Gulliver's in North Beach in 1979. The students appeared to be attempting to recreate Ken Kesey's Acid Test, as was half of the band. We played a few dates at the Sound of Music on Turk Street, in the heart of the Tenderloin. The Sound of Music made the Mabuhay look like the supper club it had once been. A dancer disrobed one night in the middle of our set before I'd even noticed she was there. I asked Celso, the unaccountably even-tempered Filipino owner what had happened to the bathroom backstage. "Too much trouble," he replied—he'd simply sheet-rocked over the door to the privy. It was the kind of place where members of the band threw things at the audience, not vice versa. Steve beaned the guy at the soundboard one night with a roll of duct tape. It did get his attention, I'll grant that. We opened there for True West, who'd driven down from Davis coasting on their 7" single recording of Syd Barrett's "Lucifer Sam." At the end of the night True West cleared $5. Our take was $3. "Nobody pay," Celso complained, stating the obvious.

Putting in 20 hours a week in the warehouse, I had the time to research how one put a record out. Independent labels run by musicians themselves were a relatively recent phenomenon, with few exceptions. But the enterprise was booming and the process surprisingly accessible. I figured out what we needed to grab from Hyde Street to get a master cut, which we were able to do in town south of Market. I pulled together a promotional mailing list from various sources and allegedly got the material copywritten while the record was being pressed, about fifteen minutes of music running at 45 RPM on 12" vinyl. Tim's spouse KB had done our artwork and it was simple and appropriately enigmatic, a line-drawing of a little gaucho on a donkey waving a tennis racket, the inaugural release of Rackit Records. We pressed 1500 copies.

We shipped hundreds of copies of *84 Rooms*—at the benign surface postal rate of $.63 a flat—to college radio stations, to commercial stations with their two hour alternative rock show each week, to the tons of print journalists then (as now) not making a living writing about music, to tiny fanzines, industry leaders, a batch of 50 to the Western Association of Rock DJs, boxes to distributors Systematic and Dutch East India. It was an odd moment—totally fly-by-night, out-of-a-shoebox operations like ours were actually getting a listen in places we never suspected we might. Billboard offered a favorable thumbnail review next to major label releases. Billy Altman at *Creem*—maybe the premiere semi-slick rock mag of the day—offered this appraisal.

> *You want goofball eclecticism? The keyboard/guitar duo of Steve Hilton and Tracy Santa manage, on this rousing little EP, to artfully spoof everything from Hot Rats era Zappa ("Camelboots") to empty brainpan rockabilly ("Cast Iron Arm") to fresh-faced British Invasion poppiness (the fifty-hooks-to-the-bar "Ask Any Girl") and they manage a belated follow-up to the Doors' "Love Street" with the oompahing Music-to-Crave-Girls-By "Candystore." Best of all is "Rings," which sounds like some Bizarroland lounge band who couldn't come up with any words to their neat surf original and just keep repeating the melody over and over instrumentally until they reach their three minute 'legal' mark.*

Altman's reading was surprisingly on the mark, other than the fact that we didn't listen to Zappa and weren't trying to spoof anything. The songs ranged as far from each other as Altman suggests, but they did in fact represent my obsessions with Mersey beat and a certain tonal approach to guitar and Steve's triangulation of Krautrock, rockabilly, and early 60s space-age muzak through his own twisted and dry sensibilities. Our live presentation was considerably more coherent and considerably rawer, but we'd gotten down in the studio the sounds we pretty much wanted to hear.

The eponymous *84 Rooms* EP had come out in early March 1983. The ripple of press and modest airplay generated opened a few doors previously closed to us. The I-Beam, a gay disco on Haight Street most nights but now booking touring alt-rock acts once a week, booked us to open for the Violent Femmes, who had just released their initial album on Slash. We went over reasonably well with a crowd frothed up over the newly ascendant Femmes, although I realized after the gig the distance between our skiffle, ska, and scum origins just a few years previous and our now more conventional rock sound. I felt like the only amateur left in the band. I also realized the amateur needed to write some new songs.

Get Drunk and Be Somebody

The I-Beam gig, news of air and club play from some surprising places, a half dozen nice print reviews from around the country. All this was enough to imagine we had some kind of future. I still regretted we weren't doing this with our initial collective, but I didn't have control over that. I'd not joined the band to be its primary songwriter. Steve was sharp and quirky in the studio and a solid rock on stage, but he was good for no more than a song or two a year.

So I wrote a half dozen new songs and they weren't half bad. The guitar-slinging chums of my youth believed that instrumental prowess and tight arrangements were the golden ticket. But at the moment and place we inhabited, our songs were our card. Though our dance club-ready tunes had been at least partially responsible for the favorable reception afforded the EP, I now dug into my roots, such as they were. I'd recorded a new song while driving across country the year before in Rock Springs, WY. Rock Springs was then a bat-shit, breakdown-lane oil boomtown, and my old high school bud Jared and Georgetown hallmate Fred Parady were doing the Lord's work outside of town for the BLM and in mining reclamation, being shot at for their trouble. During a drunken evening at Fred's I met a friend of Fred's with a basement 8-track and we put down a song the next morning. It would have served the Unstrung Heroes back in D.C. in 1974. We'd not been averse to singing the occasional Hank Williams song in the early 84 Rooms, but this was the first thing I'd written which really sounded like a country song. We rocked it up in the next 84 Rooms rehearsal, but I'd been listening to country music seriously for ten years and the seed sown had begun to fruit.

It felt like we had to hit the iron while it was at least lukewarm, and I began haranguing East Coast clubs on the phone, Ruth Polsky at Danceteria in particular. We could leverage maybe two weeks release from Jim Wade's keepers in Marin. I called George up in Boston. The Dirty Angels—the best hope among our hometown crew of climbing atop the dung heap—had crashed and burned after their A & M album. That's someone else's story to tell, but the result was no more tours opening for Aerosmith and George an unemployed, ex-rockstah guitarist. Would he mind playing guitar for us for two weeks in early December on the East Coast? Somehow I managed to string together something which seemed to make sense within the limited frame we had: 10 dates over 11 days, including stops at the Inn Square and the Rat in Boston, Danceteria and CBGBs in NYC, the Grotto in New Haven and the Living Room in Providence, the Marble Bar in Baltimore and the East Side Club in Philadelphia, and Maxwell's in Hoboken.

At the end of November we crated up my amp, my Epiphone Casino and my Fender Mustang, Steve's Farfisa, and a couple of Jim's drums and flew to New York. Borrowing a work van from the family business, we drove up to Boston for a single night of rehearsal with George, which took place in the borrowed rehearsal space of Salem

66. George, who'd stood in as bassist at an early 84 Rooms gig when Steve was out of town, was fortunately a quick study. Most of the gigs we booked demanded only a single set, but we were playing two sets a night in our two nights at the Rat.

The next afternoon we rolled our hangovers down I-95 toward New York City. I hadn't been in CBGBs in seven years, but little had changed except for a few new layers of graffiti in the men's room, which—as has been documented elsewhere—resembled a bunker in Berlin, May 1945. We drew an underwhelming Wednesday night crowd. The doorman liked us and suggested we try to book a gig with Ned Sublette. Then he distributed our door take—the doorman needed his cut, the soundman needed his $75, rain or shine, and we got the balance: $2. Two winos—meaning individuals just slightly ahead of our time line on the substance abuse schedule—joined us for a group photo under the CBGB marquee. Then we gave them our two dollars. We drove up to 110th and Broadway and squeezed our gear into the tiny elevator of the apartment building where my kind college roommate Rick had been living since 1976.

We traveled up and down I-95 and the East Coast in foul early December weather barely making gas money. It had been difficult enough to book the gigs over the phone from San Francisco with no track record other than our little five-song EP and some good press. So we weren't playing in anything like a neat, linear geographic line. But what's amazing from this distance in time is that we were booked at all. After a weekend opening for the Del Lords at the Rat, we drove nine hours from Boston in a sleet storm for our next gig at the Marble Bar in Baltimore. We established a record for being ignored that night—four paying customers—but a lovely, empathetic bartender and Unstrung Hero Bob Perilla goaded us on. We were completely freed by the virtual absence of an audience and played our loosest and best set of the tour. And, of course, over-celebrated once again—you could always count on an open bar in those days—before we poured ourselves back into the van and Bob's Orleans Street rowhouse, sharing floor space with Bob's two young kids.

Accustomed as we were to odd gigs, the East Side Club in Philadelphia was singular nonetheless. A private club rather than an open bar, the first band did not go on until 1pm. That band was the local fledgling Dead Milkmen. Their drummer Dean had yet to make 21, so while he was allowed on stage, he couldn't make himself present in the club beyond the stage. A new twist in weird bar protocol for us—we took turns bringing him beer backstage from the bar. We loaded in around 9pm then headed out on Chestnut Street for a pre-gig dinner of meatloaf and mashed potatoes at a local diner. We'd pretty much cut down to one meal a day with nights that stretched to dawn and our largely liquid diet. Tromping down the long stairway back into the basement club, someone noticed this prophetic graffiti: BANDS—YOU ARE DOOMED.

Our gig at the Living Room in Providence allowed Jim's dad and younger brother to make the short ride over from his eastern CT hometown. It also afforded us an opportunity to strike up an acquaintance with Green on Red, who we were opening for. This was the four-piece version of Green on Red—Chuck Prophet was still playing around S.F. with Eddie Porter and other folks—and the band was touring in support of its just released Slash album, *Gravity Talks*.

We had some accidental similarities—Chris Cacavas's organ was front and center in the mix and sound, as was the case with Steve's Farfisa in our quartet, and I felt pretty simpatico with Dan Stuart's random approach to lead/rhythm guitar noise. And there was our common propensity toward swill. We traded bottles of tequila and vodka back stage before and after each of our sets, further enlivened by the presence of members of the local band opening the show, Plan Nine. I recall a Howard Johnson's clam roll near New London around 3am that morning as we motored back to that night's digs in CT, so all was not blackout and debauchery. Small pleasures sustained us.

Our Danceteria gig saw us opening for synth-poppers, Our Daughter's Wedding. We were much closer in style and approach to Green on Red, but the *84 Rooms* EP read as if this might be a match, so we had no one to blame but ourselves on that front. In the months I'd been trading messages with Ruth Polsky about a potential date in the big city limelight, she at one point had us matched with a new band from England playing their first U.S. gig. Then the Smiths had to postpone their trip and appeared later that month at Danceteria.

The most salient fact regarding the Danceteria gig is that we indulged at a Cuban-Chinese diner prior to the gig. I'd been wanting a taste of this exotic cross-hatching of culinary traditions ever since I'd read the tale years before of Chinese immigration to Cuba in the 1850s, later supplemented by Chinese citizens who'd fled the Japanese and Mao in the 30s and 40s, only to flee their new home in Cuba after the rise of Castro, resulting in hybrids like squid fried rice and Chinese counter service in extremely rapid and indecipherable Spanish. Wonderful food which left me with the running trots as we waited our moment on stage. Given the condition of backstage restrooms at even exulted venues such as Danceteria, this was not a good intestinal state to inhabit at that moment. I loosened my belt, tightened my sphincter, and made it through our brief opening set without exploding.

Our final East Coast gig was a weekend night at Maxwells with the Trypes. The Trypes may not ring a bell with the casual listener, but they were a huge deal to us, as they were effectively the Feelies plus one. Unknown as we were, we had a foot in the door with the band, as the Trypes' Dave Weckerman had grown up with our SF rockabilly buddy Cory, near Steve's high school stomping ground in northern NJ. But Dave proved a bit distracted. I was in awe of Feelies guitarists Mercer and Million, though Million largely played snare drum in the Trypes. The Trypes sipped soup in the hospitable basement of Maxwell's as we loaded in. We were really on a strict evening alcohol diet by now and were a bit rough around the edges after bouncing around the East Coast. I thought we played a pretty spirited set—we were certainly the only people in the room who would have known this was our final night on the road and that this was driving our plane that evening. I punted my Epiphone Casino off the low stage as we finished. Fortunately, it survived intact. Who the fuck did I think I was? Pete Townsend? The Epiphone was likely the most expensive thing I owned, as my car back in S.F. was a markedly unrestored 1963 Studebaker.

Attempting to wind down or wind up or whatever it was I imagined I was doing as I poured beer down my throat at the front bar after the Trypes set, I squeezed in next to Myrna Marcarian, a charter member of one of my favorite bands, Human Switchboard. I let slip that I'd played with the opening band, 84 Rooms. Gregarious beyond my average isolate persona, I asked her if she'd seen any of our set. She acknowledged that she had, and walked away. Bands: you are doomed.

Sweet Home Ali Baba

It was sometime after our brief snippet of road life that the experience began to be described as the Get Drunk and Be Somebody tour. It sounds like one of George's tags. He was quite eloquent during our days in the van schooling us on the basic binary exhibited across our species—scientists vs. rule-breakers—a distinction drawn from his study of professional wrestling. But "get drunk and be somebody" derived from the stage patter of Gullivers' habitue Marin Red, who would exhort his audience at the end of a set to— in thought and deed—get drunk and be somebody. We found it an attractive and useful suggestion, a custom fit. The first part of the dictum had been easily accomplished on a nightly basis during our sojourn East. Steve had remained our designated driver as he was usually the least inebriated of us. We collectively continued work on becoming somebody.

An unanticipated by-product of our road work was that we returned to S.F. a pretty tight and forceful unit on stage. Few local bands playing their own songs had the opportunity to play live to an audience (OK—an audience of four...) more than a few times a month. Years later, I listened to a cassette tape of a February 1984 performance at the cavernous Stone, across Broadway from the

Mabuhay. Shitfire—we were burning. We'd added Jim's soul review buddy Todd Swenson on second guitar. Todd could play lead if need be, but like me he was at heart a rhythm guitarist. It was a trait I admired and it significantly fattened up our sound.

It felt like we needed to record. Not just because we had an album's worth of new songs, but also because we really were no longer the band who'd released the *84 Rooms* EP a year previous. Playing out had turned us into a rock band, albeit a slightly bent one.

Tom Mallon had remained busy since we'd initially worked in his living room studio in 1980. He now had a spacious live/work loft on the sixth floor of an old warehouse on 2nd Street, not far from the China Blue rehearsal space. He'd recorded a ton of local bands and was spending copious hours with Chris Isaak and his producer Erik Jacobson piecing together Isaak's first album. He managed to squeeze us in for two six-hour sessions in February 1984. We recorded a half dozen songs pretty much live to Mallon's eight-track in the first session and minimally overdubbed and mixed the results in the second session. Jim and Todd's bandmate Albert played bass. We did two more six-hour sessions in May, this time without Albert. We had recorded an album for $600, three new songs of Steve's and nine of mine, only one dating back to the initial iteration of 84 Rooms, the remainder written since our EP.

My warehouse work was drying up. I'd been interviewed twice by the FBI about 10k's worth of Florsheim shoes disappearing off the floor of the loading dock. The folks I suspected of facilitating that had moved along, but so had most of our business. My partner Dina had had a rough year—including the passing of her mother—

and we saw a brief opportunity to cut loose for a few weeks and visit her mother's family in England. I'd just turned 30 and had yet to visit Europe.

Trippin'

I squeezed 25 copies of the *84 Rooms* EP, a few cassettes of the new Mallon recordings, and a Pignose amp into a small suitcase. With my old Sears electric guitar over my shoulder, we landed in London in torrential rain and the next day I went out to pitch *84 Rooms*. London's record sellers were skeptical, but I managed to talk one of them into holding the cache of records until I returned in a few weeks. We traveled north to visit Dina's aunt in Blackpool, then west to see the end of the known world in Cornwall. Local punks at a gig in Mousehole were impressed by our proximity to Jello Biafra at home, as well as the fact that we had supported his candidacy for mayor in S.F. in 1978. I neglected mentioning that I'd once thrown Jello down a flight of stairs for attempting to pilfer a friend's jewelry at her house party. Jello sheepishly marched back upstairs and we reconciled, but that was too much information for this crew.

We arrived in Amsterdam mid-morning after an overnight ferry to Ostende. As we walked out of the train station the drummer in a group busking in the street turned toward us, pointed a stick and said "Hey—84 Rooms!" It was Harry, who'd briefly occupied our drum chair after Tim had split. I'd pick Harry up at the hotel he inhabited down by the Sound of Music during the month of our rehearsals together.

He was a good spirit but had an unfortunate tendency to forget where we were or what we were playing in the midst of public performance. We met him later for a beer in a small dark bar reeking of centuries of tobacco.

I finally pulled my bright turquoise electric guitar out of its case in a park in Amsterdam and in Paris to busk in the subway. I was ignored. Unlike Harry, I didn't have the constitution to work the street. Once in Paris, however, I managed to arrange a lunch with Jean-Marc Folliet, the force behind Lolita Records. Lolita had been releasing a number of interesting LPs by American bands, some loosely tagged as members of LA's Paisley Underground. Other Lolita bands—like the Plimsouls—were cutting songs which might be described as garage pop, with the sensibility of tough 60s hits but none of the major label budget. This was what we'd been up to in Tom Mallon's studio earlier that year. I offered Jean-Marc a cassette of the sessions and met him the next day at the Lolita office.

Yes—he would release a record on us. He could advance us $600 for our trouble and would press 1500 copies, of which we'd receive a box of 50. We could hardly get a gig opening for visiting luminaries in our hometown. It all seemed unlikely, but I had the papers in hand. Dina and I celebrated in the neighborhood at a tiny café, Corsica Siempre, run by anarchist Corsican separatists, a bottle of cheap red wine with lunch.

Two days later we had no more cash for red wine, cheap or otherwise, despite the fact that we were paying just seven francs a night for lodging three blocks from Notre Dame. Jean Marc had not actually handed me $600—this would be forthcoming on receipt of a master tape from S.F. We counted our francs, got to the coast on a bus, and made it across the Channel. An early morning train got us to London, and we checked prices in the bucket shops on return tickets as far as New York. Not enough cash. This was in the era before we carried credit cards, of course. We'd walked through a district of music stores and pawn shops shortly after arriving in London several weeks earlier. We returned there and I sold my Sears guitar and the Pignose for the equivalent of $150. Not bad—I'd bought the guitar in S.F. for $30. We did not have enough cash for another night in London, but if we made in to Heathrow, we'd be good. We'd have to forego picking up the *84 Rooms* EPs I'd left in town—I believe that cache is still selling on Discogs. Forking over our last pounds, we were on a flight to New York later than afternoon.

Behind the Garage Door

Over the course of the first six months of 1984, simultaneous with our Mallon recordings, Tim, Steve, Buzz, and I had been conspiring to unburden ourselves of home recordings and stray studio work we'd been accumulating for some time. Tim would prove to have the steadiest ongoing life as a musician into the future. He was immediately engaged in a number of projects once he left the band at the end of 1980: dub-influenced solo stuff and quirky dance track collaborations. Steve continued to record singular covers on his primitive home gear—rockabilly numbers, deconstructed Motown and Jimmy Webb songs, and his own atmospheric instrumentals. I was particularly interested in getting some of Buzz's songs out in one form or another. He'd been the central songwriter in the original 84 Rooms, but he could not seem to gather his considerable talents to put together another band once he'd left the nest. We'd recorded a short set of his songs live in an afternoon in Mallon's studio in 1981 with my old CT buddy Stir Dudko—who lived in my walk-in closet in the Castro for a number of months that year—beating the tubs. In addition, we had some frantic early 84 Rooms rehearsal demos, unreleased Mallon recordings, and a couple of songs from a lone Exploding Pintos studio session at SFSU.

The thread connecting all 17 cuts was that at least one of the original four members of 84 Rooms was engaged. We asked friend Gary Swanson to go out into the Sunset to snap pictures of car sheds and titled the collection *Behind the Garage Door*. Rather than carefully articulate who was playing what where, we simply listed everyone involved in making noise on at least one cut, then titled the results with all the band names we'd come up with in the past and discarded. We put together a master tape, duplicated 100 cassettes, and put it out as Rackit Records 1002.

These were—as Lou Reed sang—different times. The tape was not only received but apparently listened to by a number of national media outlets. We saw reviews in *CMJ's Futures*, LA's *Music Connection*, and in the *Fortnightly Radio Report*. Hoboken-based *Matter* magazine, a national voice in alt-rock circles at the time, described *Behind the Garage Door* as:

> *Art with a capital A. Genius. The soundtrack for America run by circus clowns, opera for tenors who only breath helium. Muzak for time travelers who commute. The fave raves of Mayor McCheese. The holy Garage Grail. But don't take my word for it. In this intergalactic maelstrom of K-Mart synthesizers, Sears guitars, and Radio Shack amps, you too will find the unutterable truth for which untold millions in eons past have flung their burning bodies against the battlements in vain. Here you'll find the Godhead in the Melon Colony's moon-eyed send-up of "Down in the Boondocks" or the Exploding Pinto's bouncy "Van Gogh's Ear" or Master Cylinder's spacey synthesizer covers of "Wichita Lineman and "*

*White Christmas." The list goes on and on in this compendium of
San Francisco-area bands whose careers will go no further than the
vital core of your galloping heart. There's the Angry Young Cookies,
the Dogmen, Mighty Dog, the Poison Ivy League, Sac o' Fun, Blind
Belly Whitefish, and a whole bunch more. Get your cassette today
and be the first kid on your block to turn the world upside down.*

A bit hyperbolic, maybe. But not so out of line with other response
we received in published reviews, all favorable, all exhibiting a certain
degree of head-scratching curiosity and wonder with what we'd
patched together. In retrospect, *Garage Door* is the most complete
document of where we were going and what we were doing with
the original iteration of 84 Rooms. I said we were eclectic, didn't I?
Everywhere at once, for sure, but the tracks also displayed a common
spirit of amateurism and disciplined abandon. It takes some running
across a tight wire to be abandoned and disciplined simultaneously,
but we had the luck and sensibility to pull it off, for a time. We
were serious, but laughs were pretty central to it all—and laughter
was an element of our presentation which was out of step with our
contemporaries and met with some confusion. But we kind of liked
confusion. *Behind the Garage Door* captured a delicate mechanism, a
sand painting, a card house we built, admired, then blew down of our
own volition. We were ready teddy, but not for prime time.

Instant Shutdown

Jean-Marc followed through on the deal we'd made in Paris and got the 84 Rooms LP *Instant Sunshine* out on Lolita in May 1985, a pretty quick turnaround what with cross-Atlantic communication and shipping of tapes and photos in the pre-WAV file universe we inhabited. We again got some good press, including this blurb from Brian Griffith at Tower Records' in-house monthly *Pulse*:

> *Vinylmania does have its rewards. Once in a blue moon, a record comes out that's so thoroughly enjoyable it's, like, time to goof off all day and scan the T.V. dial for Huckleberry Hound reruns. The record is Instant Sunshine by 84 Rooms, a San Francisco-based pop quartet. This un's so good it could make your most cynical rock critic-type strip off his zapatas and trip the light fantastic—talking the congobongo here—on the nearest tabletop. Kinda like the early Blasters, 'cause Tracy Santa whips out some spiff rockabilly guitar riffs, but with the lightness of '77 period Talking Heads, the goofy spirit of Supersnazz-era Flamin' Groovies, and the crazed hipster panache of Don Ho and vintage Sir Doug (yep, there's a Farfisa here). Check out the tunes like "Half-Hour Later," an oddball rockabilly ditty about the old Chinese food cliché (you know—half*

an hour later yer hungry again); "Don't Let Me Down," and the utterly infectious "Tell Me All About Her." Real, real cool.

With the possible exception of the Don Ho reference—a stretch beyond even our catholic tastes—Griffith was pretty much on top of where we were at on *Instant Sunshine*. We were in fact trying to record something which we imagined was pop, albeit pop on a $600 budget, recorded live, and mixed over the course of a day. Our songs were not impressionistic—they told stories, in their way. Our tongues were sometimes planted in our cheeks (see Steve's "World Without Dogs), but we were delivering ourselves in about as straightforward a fashion as we could.

We received a reasonable amount of press in Europe as well. My single semester of college French was stretched beyond capacity translating this stuff, but I recall one review which seemed largely flabbergast that a bunch of guys who looked like unemployed grad students could rock out so earnestly. It's true that our photo on the LP sleeve, taken during a China Blue rehearsal, makes Credence Clearwater look like the New Kids on the Block by comparison. But at the end of the day, we weren't trying to sell ourselves as hipsters or punk rockers or flannel-flying new American Western Men. I can safely say we paid a price for our indifference to image at this level. Like Eddie Hinton said: "It's a concept world." We scored a few decent gigs around town—the most memorable an opening slot reuniting us with Green on Red at the Berkeley Square. But I felt we needed to take to the road again. We were never hometown heroes, and we played out so sporadically that response was frequently along the lines of—"you guys are still together?"

I began to scare up out-of-town gigs on the phone. The hill seemed a bit steeper two years on—there weren't any more clubs, but there seemed to be a lot more bands with high profile record releases. My idea was that we would tour as a trio—Steve, Jim, and I—and maybe pick up George for some East Coast dates. In the course of three weeks, we'd travel up the coast to Portland and Seattle, haul ass across the top of the country with a stops in Minneapolis and Chicago, blitz the East Coast, and drop south to New Orleans and Texas before finishing out in Arizona and southern California. Way more ambitious than the Get Drunk and Be Somebody tour, but Jim had a new minivan which seemed as if it might support this round trip.

Until it turned out Jim himself could not support the roundtrip. The three of us were all working temp jobs—Steve worked for an AV company, and I split my time now teaching weekend reading classes and taking on legal temp work downtown. But Jim was a drummer in some demand beyond our little enterprise, and he had taken up paralegal work in addition—hence the minivan. He knew we would make zero profit touring the country for three weeks with 84 Rooms. It was just too much pro bono for him.

I wished he had explained this position prior to my running up hundreds of dollars in phone charges and securing some tentative dates. The one date I had locked in was a Friday and Saturday at the Central Tavern in Seattle.

More out of spite than good sense, I insisted we honor the commitment. The three of us piled gear into Jim's van and hit the road for

14 hours north, arriving in time for Friday night's sound check. We were pretty good that weekend—playing as a trio opened up space for the three of us, and I had some new songs as well. All three of us could sing, we could sing together, and we'd been playing together in one form or another for almost nine years. We talked up a few curious new fans, sucked down as much Northwestern homebrew as we could, and checked into our cheap hotel early Saturday morning, then spent a drizzly Seattle Saturday as hungover tourists in town. We played our Saturday set and hit the road again. We'd collected $300 for two nights—a good paycheck by our standards, but just enough to cover gas, food, and lodging.

Despite the new songs and the musical strength of our debut as a trio, the future was a cul-de-sac. Strip out Jim and we were no longer a band. Back to a two-legged dog. I'd booked a gig at the Hotel Utah, whose bar I'd leaned against for hundreds of hours. They rarely booked music, but had a lovely back room and stage which occasionally opened to performances. I sold them on the idea of a finale, and sold Buzz and Tim on the idea of putting together a vehicle for Buzz's songs as our opening act. That one-off aggregation—the Whiskey Worms—opened for the three-piece 84 Rooms on the first weekend of 1986. I was working a huge corporate case with scores of other paralegal temps downtown. Temp paralegal work was favored employment of the indigent artistic class in San Francisco then—writers, actors, musicians, blocked academics—we had them all, and many made the gig. Wow—you really play music, don't you, they exclaimed afterwards. Yeah—you caught us heading out the door. Thanks for coming.

How Can I Miss You?

I felt a great burden lifted and an expansive absence. The final gig had brought the four original members of 84 Rooms together in an act of closure. But we had some loose ends dangling and felt compelled to play with those strings, pulling together a final Rackit Records release, *I Bury Ringo*, a 7" vinyl EP. Steve, Jim, and I had recorded two final 84 Rooms songs that fall, one a cover of the Fugs "C.I.A. Man." That led the A-side. Two of Buzz's songs that we'd recorded on Tim's 8-track reel-to-reel filled in two more slots. That fall I'd also gone into Tim's basement for an afternoon and recorded four of my new songs fully solo, the first (and last) time I'd ever play drums on a recording. I say drums, but it was only a kick drum and snare, as that was the most gear I could handle and expect to remain relatively syncopated. A song from that session rounded out the EP. As with *Behind the Garage Door*, we conveniently attributed the three non-84 Rooms tunes to spurious groups, *der* Love Nuts and the Idlewiles. Suggesting anything was a solo effort—even when one person played and sang everything on the track—was beyond our conceptual framework.

Even with this modest hodge-podge, our luck with favorable reviews in national publications continued. We were apparently a critic's band, because we sure weren't selling records. Scott Jackson in *Option* described *Ringo* as

> *Four off-kilter perspectives from three bands: 84 Rooms, der Love Nuts, and the Idelwiles. The one common denominator is Tracy Santa on vocals and guitar. Light, funny, a little demented and very tuneful, these tracks go down like a Fizzie: pop, pop, fizz. Tracy's Roy Orbison-influenced vocals on "Maybe Tomorrow" are a treat. The cover by 84 Rooms of the Fugs' "C.I.A. Man" rollicks along like a top 40 hit in an alternative universe. Der Love Nuts are lovely, in a bent sort of way. Slight and perhaps lost on their own set of radio waves, these tracks are drenched in spirit and charm.*

Again, we were fortunate to have listeners who heard and sensed what we were up to. As with our two earlier Rackit Records releases, we were pegged as playing in and appealing to an alternative universe and listeners there situated. We were unfortunately also trying to appeal to consumers in the world we inhabited. *Instant Sunshine* may have done a better job in that regard, but I have an ongoing affection for the skew Rackit material. Benoit Binet in the French rock mag *Nineteen* finished his review of *I Bury Ringo* by stating that

> "*Quez vous aimez les Blasters ou Captain Beefheart, Mink Deville ou les Everly Brothers, ce disque est fait pour vous. Musique nature pour gens nature.*"

Not sure if we were playing for celestial vagabonds or the natural man. Just another squad of lost planet airmen by the San Francisco Bay.

Last Rites

Buzz and I did a gig as the Beverage Brothers, opening for Mark Eitzel and Penelope Houston at an all-acoustic show, but it was a one-off. I had a handful of new songs but was not quite sure what to do with them. I'd established that my music had a certain appeal, but that none of that appeal translated to cash. I was working downtown as a low level legal drone. I'd occasionally get a review printed in the *S.F. Examiner's* Sunday book review section and all the lawyers thought I was the cat's meow, living the life of Reilly. Meanwhile, Reilly spent afternoons digging through the financial records of a bottomless RICO case. I'd worked as a junior high teacher's assistant in S.F. public schools and as a tutor at the juvenile lock-up while at SFSU, had taught two summers and occasional weekends for the Institute of Reading Development, and I began poking at the idea of going back to school to actually learn something about teaching.

But I couldn't kick playing. I booked time in an attic studio near my place on Potomac Street in the lower Haight and went in for an evening with Jim Wade. We cut three songs, one a cover of Nick Drake's "Fly." Simple, quick overdubs, including me on two-fingered organ, a first. Jim was not only the best musician in any group I shared with him but usually the best keyboard player. But some arrangements—most, in the case of my songs—demand a degree of both stupidity and simplicity, which was also why I played bass on my own recordings. It was just too much work to get a real bass player to dummy down their approach. Better to start with a real dummy.

When two of the three songs from this four-hour session came out the next year on the German Exile label, David Stubbs in the British weekly *Melody Maker* described the results as sounding "*Like R.E.M. in a telephone kiosk in the Nevada desert, at once personal and remote.*" Fair enough—the studio we'd recorded in was not that much bigger than a phone booth. Scott McCaughey elaborated at slightly greater length in Seattle's *The Rocket*.

Tracy comes out of the eclectic San Francisco group 84 Rooms, whose Instant Sunshine LP on Lolita (France) is immensely enjoyable. Santa's own "Hell in a Handtruck" sounds more uplifting than its lyric—the minimalist-crude but melodic-Beau Brummelsian approach serves to put the weight on the superb vocals, where it belongs. The flip is a conceptually elegant cover of the ever-uplifting Nick Drake's "Fly." It feels perfect and eerie like the way "Endless Sleep" polished off Nick Lowe's Bowi UP. Get it.

A few kind words. It's amazing the degree to which a sympathetic reading of your work can fuel you for another year of out-of-pocket basement and attic recordings, for another round of splitting $50 four ways at a Wednesday night gig. Minimalist-crude but conceptually elegant. The story of our past nine years in five words.

Putting together another band to play my stuff just seemed more than I could do. My last few gigs in San Francisco brought me full circle to the sort of dates we'd played nine years earlier, before I'd begun writing. The circle extended back to junior high school, really. The Abbey Tavern was an Irish bar out in San Francisco's avenues on Van Ness. It was colorful—the kind of place where my partner (now spouse) Dina was accused by a fellow patron of snorting his coke off the urinal in the men's room. Now—that's ambitious, or evidence of a strong jones on Dina's part. The band we set up with once a month was basically the Exploding Pintos without Nadine, our Gulliver's band—Jim Gordon, Gary Arago, Jim Wade and I. We never rehearsed and vowed to play at least a few songs we simply heard on the radio on the way over, as long as they were songs we didn't actually know. Jim would sing Crazy Elephant's "Gimme Gimme Good Lovin'," from behind the drums, Jim Gordon a couple of Merle Haggard songs he'd learned from the Grateful Dead. We had a soft spot for songs off *Exile on Main Street* and Toots and the Maytals' "Peepin' Tom." The stage was narrow and pointed toward the rest of the bar like the bow of a ship, about three feet above the small dance floor. We had to set up in single file, so that everyone was looking at the back of my head up front. I would play electric mandolin on "Stray Cat Blues," with Jim Gordon on vocals, making like Brian Jones on sitar.

One night a fight broke out between Irish factions and lasted for three songs. We finally broke into "All You Need Is Love" and didn't stop until the ruckus did. Maybe it was all about cocaine being snorted off the urinal rather than politics or religion. We never found out. The primary casualty was our Rastafarian friend who took a beer bottle to the head trying to break things up.

We would play four sets at the Abbey Tavern, and one night I ran cassettes in my boombox on top of my Ampeg ReverbeRocket amp for most of the night. We would alternate calling ourselves Biffo the Bear or the Bloody Holly Experience—I'm not sure who we were that night. But the tapes, as rough and unbalanced as the sound was going to be up on our narrow sloop of a stage, are some of my favorite recordings. We played none of my songs—that was not fare the Abbey Tavern crowd came to hear. But we played with the comfort of having worked with each other for almost a decade, with a good deal of joy and little ego, careening song to song without a set list, not really caring or trying to reproduce anything like a facsimile of the original recording, three of the four of us singing what we remembered as we remembered it if we remembered it. The tape evidences some real power from time to time. The BeeGees, NRBQ, Gram Parsons, the Stones, the Velvet Underground—we mashed them all up. For those moments, our lives were still being saved by rock and roll.

Defying most odds, in April the one grad school application I'd posted proved fruitful. We would move back East. I bought an Econoline van for $600 from Tim's neighbor and put another $600 into equipping it with brakes and getting three of four gears working. You did not so much pour oil into the engine as pour it over the engine. The van would prove to demand one quart of oil per 100 miles across the country, thirty quarts to New York. Dina and I loaded out our Potomac Street apartment into the van. San Francisco was just getting too expensive for us—we were carrying $700 a month rent split four ways with our other two roommates.

In early August we climbed up front in the Econoline and pulled slowly out of the neighborhood. We were loaded to the tits, to the roof, an antique night table between the front seats. I gingerly shifted into second gear as we ascended Fillmore towards Oak Street. As I let up on the clutch as the red light at Page turned to green, we popped a wheelie, the front of the van a foot off the ground as we inched forward. I felt like I was back on a banana seat bike, ten years old. With 3000 miles in front of us, the likelihood of making it across the Bay Bridge seemed very low. We sped forward—and backwards to the East—at 40 mph.

Epilogue

Get Into My Cloud

The first time I saw the future of rock and roll (or was it my rock and roll future?) I was 12. I saw it on the Clay Cole Show after school and it wore a turban.

Sam "the Sham" Samudio remains an undervalued original. And a counterfeit from the get-go. He and his Pharaohs did not walk like Egyptians. He copped to this right up front: Sam *the Sham*. And who would bother arguing the power of "Wooly Bully?"

But just what is "Wooly Bully" about?

The song came out in June 1965. School had just ended—I was picking strawberries for the old Yankee lady, Mrs. Wisner Wilson, and her roadside farm stand. Seven cents a quart to underage seasonal help. We'd graft the good parts of two partially rotten strawberries together with a piece of straw. Chuck fully rotten strawberries at each other, so that by the end of the day our white T-shirts were red. I had a new red transistor radio with a little earplug, so I could listen to the Top 40 countdown on WICC 630 on the AM dial out of Bridgeport, CT every night after I went to bed.

Hattie told Maddie/about a thing she saw
Two big horns/and a wooly jaw

For years I thought Sam Samudio was saying

Two big whores/and a wooly doll.

That made as much sense as anything to me. That's how I sang it
nights at Gullivers in 1979. So try this on.

*I live on a cloud
And all the night,
Night, night
Fallin' around my block*

*I sit at home,
And lookin' out the
Window and imagin'
It's the world outside,*

*And inside,
The guys all dressed,
Up to start,
The union drive,*

*Cause I walked,
By and I found out that,
I had the time out,
To give her a good time,*

*Hey, Hey, He, He,
Get off of my cloud,
Hey Hey, He, He,
Get off of my cloud,*

Hey, Hey, He, He,
Get off of my cloud,
Gonna ran on,
Through the crowd,

The tompo
Of the ringin'
I say the high speed,
Was there all of the time,

It might have taken you a moment to realize you were reading the lyrics for the Rolling Stones 1965 hit "Get Off of My Cloud." The lyrics come from an insert in a London Records Japanese release of a double A-side single, "Satisfaction" on one side, "Get Off of My Cloud" on the other.

Oddly enough, the lyrics offered for "Satisfaction" are a spot-on translation of Jagger's muckled delivery. But the translation of "Get Off My Cloud" just gets weirder the further into it you go. What the translator heard as Jagger begins the song's final verse is

Pick a time,
put up with it,
Kind of dangerous,
Slide right down,

Whereas what Jagger seems to be saying, if one is a native speaker of English

I was sick and tired
Fed up with this

And decided
To take a drive downtown

You don't have to be Japanese to get it so wrong. My ex-spouse Dina insisted that Steppenwolf's John Kay was sending us a warning in "Born to Be Wild"

Buy all your guns at discount/Explode in your face.

This reminds me of how we used to spend the second half of our lunch period for most of my sophomore year in high school. Latin class followed lunch. This was an honors section of Latin—who knows how most of us ingrates ended up in an honors class after freshman year, though it may have had to do with our freshman Latin teacher Father Sullivan, who would later head out to Jesuit alcohol rehab. But not before asserting that having learned to decline the verb "to be," we now "knew all of Latin." Good—that's where we stopped. We spent the rest of the year with Father Sullivan taking entire class periods interrogating single lines of Ovid, such as "a pillow is helpful in the art of love." What was that about, we asked. Father Sullivan tried to explain, but he didn't try very hard. In second year honors Latin we were with Father Welch, who wrote the textbook we were using. He demanded something beyond the declension of "to be," and had us translating a chapter of Caesar's *Gallic Wars* each day.

This was of course way more work that we were willing to tolerate. So we divvied it up—maybe two or three of us actually worked to translate a given chapter, and the rest of us took notes and basically copied out the results. With fifteen of us in the class, this way you really only had to work on one chapter a week. This is now termed collaborative learning, I think.

We gathered in an empty classroom one day after lunch collaboratively learning on a chapter titled "Hannibal Outwits the Cretans." I know that sounds too good to be true, but there we were. Some of us had actually picked up a bit of Latin, more by osmosis than through any conscious effort. Perrotti was one of the worker bees that day, a good-natured Italian kid, didn't rock the boat, not out to cause anyone any harm. Did I mention that Degenerate Jim and Cave N. were members of this cabal?

So Perrotti is trotting out his translation. All good so far with Hannibal and the Cretans. Then Perrotti gets to a line, translating a statement of Hannibal's as "He saw his holiday from five miles away."

What the fuck?

Perrotti, would you repeat that?

"He saw his holiday from five miles away." With Perrotti's CT accent, it comes out as *sore* his holiday, but we heard it right the first time.

Really, Perrotti? "He saw his holiday from five miles away?" What the fuck is that supposed to mean?

We couldn't get a damned thing done for the rest of the period. We just couldn't get beyond Perrotti's reading of Caesar.

It was visionary. Cave N. was rolling on the floor in hysterics. Degenerate Jim bent over his desk, gasping for air. Our collective jaws had to be winched back to our upper plates. We had some fun with Father Welch when class started. The previous week we had pressed him to help us say, in Latin: *I came, I saw, I killed myself.* He was having none of it that day, and set us straight regarding Hanni-bal and the Cretans, with the proper translation and a grimace. But the damage was done. We'd crossed the muddy ditch. *He saw his holiday from five miles away.* It's virtually the only thing I recall from that year of Latin.

I have a similar relationship with this imaginative translation of Jagger/Richards. I'm stuck on—fascinated with—lost in: the wrongness of it all.

> *The tompo of the ringin'*
> *I say the high speed*
> *Was there all the time*

I like the Jagger/Richards' lyric. It's a funny story. But the Japanese translation is like a Zen koan. We're never going to get to the bottom of it. And that's OK.

Rock and roll has always seemed to me to be about making it up as you go, and then never getting to the bottom of it. Just what *were* the Kingsmen saying in "Louie Louie"? Or you want to be a bunch of Egyptians, and you're from Dallas or Memphis—knock yourself out. And it's about being OK with getting it wrong. *He saw his holiday from five miles away.* As one possible translation of Caesar's account of outwitting the Cretans, this version offers its own rewards. It's faking it until you're making it, but then realizing faking it is a pretty good move too, and maybe as close as you're going to get to making it.

Or: check the *Oxford English Dictionary*. Tom Po n. [perhaps shortened < Tom Poker, n.]. Obsolete rare (the name of) a ghost; *a bogeyman*; cf. Tom Poker, n.

The *ghost* of the ringing? Or —Tom Po: the boogie man.

> *I'm going to boogie with the doctor*
> *Going to boogie with the nurse*
> *Going to keep on boogeyin'*
> *'Til they throw me in the hearse*
> —Doctor Ross, "Boogie Disease"

The tempo of the ringing. The high speed was there all the time. What does it mean that the high speed was there all the time? Always an option? Always an opportunity? A sixth gear? High speed as the source of an impulse to play rock and roll, the desire to write (or rewrite or revise) rock and roll songs, to listen incessantly for years and years, decade after decade, long after you should have moved on from childish things, gathering with others in the pursuit of creating and playing a rock and roll song from scratch? Is that even possible? The version of "House of the Rising Sun" we were playing in Ricky Ziegler's living room as seventh-graders was as much an act of creation as any song I've written since, but it sure wasn't from scratch.

Where you dreamed you might be in the beginning is where you end up, if you're lucky. But just to be part of a process is what we always sought. The process is the star attraction, the headliner, the reason to be (still) at it. Did the Rolling Stones continue to play "Get Off of My Cloud" to stadium crowds into their dotage for the money? Sure they did. But they've got plenty of money. I bet they are sometimes excited about simply getting together and well, rehearsing. Having a few laughs at no one's expense. Tapping the high speed for their own sake and for the joy of it.

Leaving San Francisco I turned a corner, albeit on two wheels. Had I put childish things behind me? A bit. I had through experience determined that making a living as a musician was not going to happen. In other words, another unsuccessful musician.

Is that right? An unsuccessful musician? A sham? Or is the mere act of playing music together the success, creating something out of silence and untuned strings?

It was hardly a blink from blowing up my Tiger amp to parting the Irish Sea at the Abbey Tavern. A Boy Scout patrol, a campout with a lifetime of smoking in a day, purloined whiskey from a jar—a Gerber Baby food jar, in my case. Eggs cooked over a newspaper fire in the rainy morning.

Like a Rolling Stone, I miss rehearsing for life's performances. Making it up, gluing together found objects, borrowed melodies, half phrases of someone else's tune, bits of ourselves, a little nakedness revealed. It was all a rehearsal, from Greg White's basement and "Little Tin Soldier" on.

Playing music together is an expression of hope. If you can claim to be rehearsing, you're still becoming. After a while we rehearsed on stage. Became in public. Jazz musicians call it improvisation, but we never imagined we had that kind of talent, and we were mostly right. Our *tompo* was sometimes off.

Sam's Pharaohs chanted behind him, "Oh—*that's bad*." Sam the Sham replied: "No—that's *good*," I side with the Sham.

ACKNOWLEDGMENTS

Playing music is a team sport. Writing can seem a solo bid by comparison, but none of these pages would have seen the light without every individual mentioned therein. We all know how subjective and selective memory can be, and as a work of recollection, my account no doubt sports omissions and distortions of objective reality which I'm incapable of rectifying. But as Alfred Jarry suggested on that T-shirt long ago in the Haight, objective reality can be overrated. I nonetheless apologize for any and all misrepresentations. These faults are mine and I own them fully.

If nothing else, this brief account afforded me time with some folks who likely never understood how dear they were to me. I think especially of those for whom this message has come too late: Rick Dormer, Rob Georgia, Bob Griffin, Charlie Karp, Jim Pisaretz, Cory Shepard, Jim Stellar, Jim Wade, and Joey Wirsing among them. These friends have exited our sphere but are with me and in these pages, at heart.

I did not actually stop playing music or writing and singing my songs on crossing the Bay Bridge headed east at the age of 33. But that's another story. Among those individuals in unwritten acts I particularly want to note John Howerton and Jamie Phillips (in Somerville), Lisa Mednick, Bill Conley, Dave Clements, Paul Henehan, Donald Saaf, Warren Zanes, Carey Corson, Jordan Cook, and Al Tharp (in New Orleans), Christoph Hahn, Steffi Long, and Wolfgang Doebeling (in Berlin), Maarten Schiethart, Nick Phillips, and Jerker Emanuelson (in the Netherlands, Australia, and Sweden) and Michael Salkind, Nathan Archer, Chuck Snow, and Dan Nelson (in Colorado Springs). I took plenty of time away from music in the years after leaving San Francisco, but I never quite shook the bug. Thanks to all who helped keep the channel open.

Friends and family were absolutely central to finishing my brief narrative, one which had been germinating for many years. Peter Shwartz offered me crucial editorial advice when I most needed it. He was never (almost never...says Peter) wrong. Steve Woodhams, another old SFSU friend, offered encouragement at just the right moment. Bill Henderson, proprietor of the world's smallest and most smartly stocked bookstore, in Sedgwick, Maine, gave me a generous push. Rob Dudko was always there to talk about music and what it all might mean. Donald Anderson, author of memoirs that put mine in the shade, has long been a key mentor. Old friends Kevin Berger, Sean Elder, and Gina Arnold from San Francisco's *WARD Report* were there years ago when I began groping my way toward writing about music. Bebe and Maggie Santa-Wood and Dina Wood have always offered unconditional and unstinting support. Partner-in-life Quatie Bryan made me the space and gave me the time to finally bring this short story home.

My story incorporates appraisals, criticism, snippets of lyrics throughout. I have attributed sources as carefully as possible, but I want to acknowledge here the contributions of Billy Altman, Brian Griffith, Scott McCaughey, Scott Jackson, and Benoit Binet in fleshing out response to our under-the-radar releases.

Warren Zanes has had my back since loaning us a drum kit in New Orleans for the 1989 SXSW. His foreword is of that piece. Finally, I am grateful to Don Kallaus for his capacity to see something in this narrative, fashion it into a handsome book, and bring it out on Rhyolite.

AUTHOR'S NOTE

Tracy Santa is a recovering academic. His recent recordings with the Wild Hares on Pill Pauper Records can be accessed on Bandcamp. He lives in Maine and Arizona.

You, too, can go to Bandcamp!